KT-524-122

Left **Visitor on a raft at Khao Sok National Park** Right **Nightlife in Patong**

Museums and Monuments	50
Restaurants	54
Bars and Nightclubs	56
Entertainment Venues	58
Outdoor Activities	60
Marine Activities	62
Children's Activities	64
Markets and Shopping Areas	66
Places to Buy Souvenirs	68
Day Trips	70

Around Phuket

The South	74
The North	82
Farther Afield	92

Streetsmart

Planning Your Trip	102
Getting There and Around	103
Security and Health	104
Banking and Communications	105
Sources of Information	106
Things to Avoid	107
Budget Tips	108
Accommodation and Dining Tips	109
Specialist Holidays	110
Etiquette Tips	111
Luxury Hotels	112
Boutique Hotels	113
Romantic Hotels	114
Mid-Range Hotels	115
Budget Hotels	116
Family Hotels	117
General Index	118
Acknowledgments	124
Phrase Book	126

Left **Visitors relaxing on beach chairs, Kata Beach** Right **Elephant trekking at Naiharn**

Key to abbreviations
Adm *admission* **B** *Baht*

3

TOP **10**
PHUKET

WILLIAM BREDESEN

C015819229

Left *Muay thai* fight, Patong Center **Big Buddha** Right **Dragon pillars, Tha Rua Shrine**

DK

LONDON, NEW YORK,
MELBOURNE, MUNICH AND DELHI
www.dk.com

Printed and bound in China by
South China Printing Co. Ltd

First published in the UK in 2012
by Dorling Kindersley Limited,
80 Strand, London WC2R 0RL
A Penguin Random House Company

14 15 16 17 10 9 8 7 6 5 4 3 2 1

**Copyright 2012, 2014 © Dorling
Kindersley Limited, London**

Reprinted with revisions 2014

A CIP catalogue record is available from the
British Library

ISBN 978 1 40932 684 7

Within each Top 10 list in this book, no
hierarchy of quality or popularity is implied.
All 10 are, in the editor's opinion,
of roughly equal merit.

MIX
Paper from
responsible sources
FSC
www.fsc.org   FSC™ C018179

Contents

Phuket's Top 10

Phuket's Highlights	6
Phuket Town	8
Wat Chalong	12
Patong	14
Khao Phra Thaeo National Park	16
Sirinat National Park	18
Naiharn Beach	20
Kata Beach	22
Similan Islands National Park	24
Khao Sok National Park	26
Phang Nga Bay	30
Moments in History	34
Buddhist Temples	36
Chinese Shrines	38
Beaches	40
Viewpoints	42
Picturesque Places	44
Scenic Walks	46
Fairs and Festivals	48

PHUKET'S TOP10

Phuket's Highlights
6–7

Phuket Town
8–11

Wat Chalong
12–13

Patong
14–15

Khao Phra Thaeo
National Park
16–17

Sirinat National Park
18–19

Naiharn Beach
20–21

Kata Beach
22–23

Similan Islands
National Park
24–25

Khao Sok
National Park
26–29

Phang Nga Bay
30–31

PHUKET'S TOP 10

📷10 Phuket's Highlights

Phuket's extraordinary tropical setting needs little introduction. The marvelous white-sand beaches, rolling green hills, and tranquil emerald and turquoise waters have lured visitors for centuries. But the island boasts more than sublime beaches. Phuket and its surrounding areas are also home to pristine national parks, wildlife sanctuaries, and scuba diving sites, while cultural highlights include Buddhist temples, museums, shrines, and historic architecture.

Phuket Town
Magnificent architecture, Chinese shrines, bustling outdoor marketplaces, and authentic local cuisine are all available at Phuket's cultural heart *(see pp8–11)*.

Wat Chalong
Phuket's most important Buddhist temple features sacred sculptures and imagery, and the Grand Pagoda houses a bone fragment of the Buddha *(see pp12–13)*.

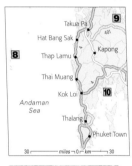

Khao Phra Thaeo National Park
Home to jungle trekking trails, waterfalls, and exotic animals and plants, this national park boasts a wealth of natural attractions. The park also has a Gibbon Rehabilitation Centre *(see pp16–17)*.

Patong
Wild and uninhibited, Patong is the island's busiest tourist beach and home to a large number of hotels, restaurants, and nightlife venues. This is the ideal spot for people who want to be in the middle of the action *(see pp14–15)*.

Sirinat National Park
Located along Phuket's pristine northwest coast, Sirinat National Park grants protection to a large area of undeveloped beachfront, as well as the island's last mangrove forest. There are a number of upscale hotels here *(see pp18–19)*.

Takua Pa
Hat Bang Sak
Thap Lamu
Thai Muang
Kok Loi
Thalang
Phuket Town
Kapong
Andaman Sea
Nai Thon
Bang Tao Bay
Kamala Bay
Andaman Sea
Karon
miles 0 km 30

Preceding pages Ton Sai Waterfall, Khao Phra Thaeo National Park

Naiharn Beach

6 This idyllic white-sand beach on Phuket's southern tip is framed by rolling hills and provides one of the island's most picturesque tropical backdrops. Don't miss the fabulous view from the sunset viewpoint at Phromthep Cape *(see pp20–21)*.

Kata Beach

7 Once a hippie haven, Kata is today home to upscale resorts and hotels, and is a favorite with couples and families. The gorgeous beach and turquoise waters are the area's main draw *(see pp22–3)*.

Similan Islands National Park

8 The waters surrounding the Similan Islands provide incredible visibility, ideal for viewing exotic marine life such as colorful fish, staggering reefs, and dramatic underwater rock formations, making it one of the world's favorite scuba diving destinations *(see pp24–5)*.

Khao Sok National Park

9 At the heart of this spectacular national park are ancient evergreen forests, majestic limestone mountains, and Cheow Laan Lake, where you can rest in floating bamboo-raft houses *(see pp26–9)*.

Phang Nga Bay

10 Staggering limestone cliffs jut up from this bay, where world-famous sights include James Bond Island and the magnificent Ko Phi Phi. You can explore the water tunnels, caves, and uninhabited islands by kayak *(see pp30–31)*.

Map labels:
Kung Bay · 4005 · 6002 · Po Bay · Bang Rong · Muang Mai · alang · Na Sat · 4027 · Bang Rong Bay · Ko Kaeo · Sapam Bay · 3013 · Ko Maphrao · thu · 402 · Ratsada · ong · 1 · Phuket Bay · 2 · Ao Makham · Chalong Bay · Cape Phanwa · Ko Lon · wai

miles 0 km 5

TOP 10 Phuket Town

The historical and administrative center of Phuket traces its roots back centuries – first, to the early European traders and later to the Chinese immigrants who arrived here during the local tin mining boom of the 19th century. Today, Phuket Town continues to thrive as one of the island's most authentic cultural areas, punctuated by magnificent architectural treasures, Chinese shrines, colorful open-air markets, and restaurants that serve some of Phuket's most delicious local cuisines.

Chatuchak Weekend Market, Phuket Town

🗸 Avoid walking tours at midday – the sun can make the streets unbearably warm.

☕ Try the iced coffee at Thungkha Kafae atop Rang Hill.

• Map K3
• Phuket Cultural Centre: 21 Thepkasatri Road; Map K2; 07622 3616; open 8:30am–4:30pm Mon–Fri; closed weekends and public hols; Adm free
• Chatuchak Weekend Market: Map P5; open 9am–6pm Sat & Sun
• Phuket Butterfly Garden and Insect World: 71/6 Moo 5, Soi Paneung, Yaowarat Road; Map K2; 07621 0861; open 9am–5pm daily; Adm B300 (adults), B150 (children aged 4–10), free (children under 4); www.phuketbutterfly.com

Top 10 Features

1 Marvelous Architecture
2 Phuket Vegetarian Festival
3 Phuket Cultural Centre
4 Chatuchak Weekend Market
5 Chinese Shrines
6 Monkey Hill
7 Ko Sirey
8 Suan Luang Park
9 Rang Hill
10 Phuket Butterfly Garden and Insect World

1 Marvelous Architecture

The distinctive architectural style found in many of Phuket Town's old mansions *(below)* and shop houses derives from the British colonial style, once popular in Malaysia and Singapore *(see pp10–11)*.

2 Phuket Vegetarian Festival

This annual festival is held over nine days in late September/early October. Devotees perform shocking rituals of self-mutilation, as they plunge spears, swords, and more through their flesh.

3 Phuket Cultural Centre

Located on the Rajabhat University campus, this museum houses old Thai shadow puppets, tin mining artifacts, historic photographs, and a range of books on Phuket's culture and history.

4 Chatuchak Weekend Market

With a wide range of clothes, decorative items, trinkets, souvenirs, and delicious food, this open-air bazaar on the southern side of Phuket Town is definitely worth a visit.

Chinese Shrines

Vibrant and colorful artwork can be seen at Chinese temples throughout the town. The shrines *(left)* play an important role during the Chinese New Year and the annual Chinese Vegetarian Festival.

Monkey Hill

Although the views from the summit of nearby Rang Hill are more impressive, Monkey Hill offers a somewhat more unique experience – curious hordes of macaque monkeys *(right)* congregate near the hilltop. Watch your belongings – the monkeys may try to snatch them from you.

Ko Sirey

Linked to Phuket Town via a small bridge, Sirey Island *(main image)* features hilly forest trails that wind through rubber plantations. Along the coasts, you will find pristine views and restaurants serving delicious fresh seafood at very low prices. Located on a hill, Ko Sirey temple enjoys sea views and features a large reclining Buddha image in its main hall.

Phuket Butterfly Garden and Insect World

This conservation and research facility breeds some 40 unique butterfly species, many of which are reintroduced into the wild. Visitors can also witness the stunning transformation of more than 6,000 larvae into butterflies each month.

Suan Luang Park

Also known as King Rama IX Park, this pleasant garden comes alive in the early mornings, when people come to exercise and perform Tai Chi. The park boasts lotus ponds and a walking path *(below)*.

Rang Hill

Wonderful views of Phuket Town can be enjoyed from the summit of Rang Hill, where a breezy, tree-shaded park also provides a relaxing venue for picnics, exercise, or reading a book.

Origins of the Vegetarian Festival

In 1825, a traveling Chinese opera company performing in Kathu, Phuket, contracted malaria. According to legend, the afflicted nursed themselves back to health by observing a strict vegetarian diet to purify their minds and bodies, and to honor the nine Emperor Gods of Chinese Taoism. They recovered, and the first Vegetarian Festival was held to praise and thank the gods.

Left **Blue Elephant Restaurant** Center **THAI Airways Office building** Right **Phuket Provincial Hall**

TOP 10 Historic Buildings in Phuket Town

1 Chinpracha House

This 19th-century mansion has served as a backdrop for several Hollywood films including Oliver Stone's 1993 movie, *Heaven and Earth*, based on the Vietnam War. Today, open to the public as a museum, the house stands as a timeless reminder of an earlier era. ⊗ *98 Krabi Road • Map N5 • 07621 1281 • Open 9am–4:30pm Mon–Sat, 9am–2:30pm Sun • Adm*

2 Standard Chartered Bank

The country's oldest foreign bank was formerly housed inside this graceful two-story Straits Settlement building. Efforts are ongoing to convert it into a public museum. ⊗ *Corner of Phuket Road and Phang Nga Road • Map P5*

3 Dibuk Grill and Bar

Another fine example of century-old architecture, this building now serves as a relaxing eatery known for its delicious Thai and French cuisine. The old Chinese-style house features soft interior lighting and antique fans. ⊗ *69 Dibuk Road • Map P5 • 07621 8425 • Open 11am–11pm Mon–Sat*

4 Phuket Thai Hua Museum

Built in the early 20th century, this distinctive building was once used as a schoolhouse. Today a museum, it continues to house student artifacts such as old books, desks, and photographs. It is also used for private functions and exhibitions. ⊗ *Thalang Road • Map P5 • 07621 1224 • Open 9am–5pm daily • closed public holidays • Adm • http://thaihuamuseum.com*

5 Phuket Provincial Hall

The first Phuket building to receive a national conservation award, the Provincial Hall was built in the early 1910s. It originally featured 99 doors and no windows, and is said to be the first reinforced concrete building in Thailand. ⊗ *Narisorn Road • Map Q4 • 07635 4875 • Open 9am–5pm daily*

Entrance to the China Inn Café and Restaurant

6 China Inn Café and Restaurant

Exquisite wooden doors, Chinese lanterns, and tiled floors decorate the entrance of this classic Straits Settlement style house. The interior showcases a wonderful collection of old Chinese artifacts, while the highly regarded dining space is set in the backyard. ✪ *20 Thalang Road • Map P5 • 07635 6239 • Open 11am–5pm Mon–Sat*

House of the Beautiful Images

Located on Soi Rommani, a charming street lined with wonderful old architecture on both sides, the House of the Beautiful Images today serves as a café specializing in breakfast and coffee. The space also exhibits photography. ✪ *Soi Rommani 12 • Map P5 • 07621 4207 • Open 10am–9pm Thu–Tue • Closed Wed*

Facade of the House of the Beautiful Images

Phuket Philatelic Museum

Also known as the Post Office Museum, this 20th-century building has displays detailing the history of the Thai postal service. ✪ *Montri Road • Map P5 • 07621 1020 • Open 9:30am–5:30pm Tue–Sat*

Blue Elephant Restaurant

Located next door to the Chinpracha House museum, this former governor's mansion is now a fine-dining venue. ✪ *96 Krabi Road • Map N5 • 07635 54355 • Open 11am–10:30pm daily*

THAI Airways Office

The airline bought this mansion in 1947. The white, two-story building continues to serve as the THAI Airways Office in Phuket Town. It is believed to have been constructed in 1922. ✪ *78 Ranong Road • Map P5 • 07636 0444 • Open 8am–5pm daily*

Top 10 Characteristics of Straits Settlement Architectural style

1. Romanesque arched colonnades (porticoes)
2. Inner courtyards (airwells)
3. Exterior windows with Romanesque arches
4. Double doors and double shutters
5. Terracotta tiled roofs
6. Tiled floors
7. Victorian ornamentation
8. Chinese signage
9. Ornamental wrought-iron gates
10. Eaves decorated with ceramic shards

Architectural Legacy

During the tin boom of the late 19th and early 20th centuries, numerous Chinese immigrants descended on Phuket seeking to capitalize on the island's newfound economic opportunities. The most successful tin barons often built gorgeous colonial-style mansions. The architectural style, known as Straits Settlements style, was derived from the British colonies in Singapore, Malacca, and Penang. Examples of this style abound in old Phuket Town, particularly in the shop houses and mansions along Dibuk, Thalang, Phang Nga, Rassada, Yaowarat, and Phuket roads.

The 19th-century Chinpracha House

Discover more at www.dk.com

Wat Chalong

Although historical records are unclear, Wat Chalong was probably first constructed during the reign of King Rama II (r.1809–24). The temple moved locations at one point, and the original structure no longer remains. Today, this complex features sacred imagery, including sculptures and mural paintings that depict the Buddha's life. The holiest object is a bone fragment of the Lord Buddha, now housed inside the Grand Pagoda. The temple is known as Wat Chaitararam by royal decree, but everybody refers to it as Wat Chalong.

The Grand Pagoda in Wat Chalong

🕑 Remember to dress conservatively and remove your shoes before entering certain buildings.

🍴 A number of street food vendors, selling everything from fried grasshoppers to grilled chicken and pork skewers marinated in chilli sauce, congregate outside the temple.

• Chao Fah Nok Road; Map J4; 07621 1036, 07638 1893; open 7am–5pm daily

Top 10 Features

1. Buddha Image
2. Grand Pagoda
3. Gilded Statues
4. Architecture
5. Wall Paintings
6. Merit-Making
7. Firecrackers
8. Fortune Telling
9. Wax Figures
10. Temple History

Buddha Image

Known as Poh Than Jao Wat, the temple's principal Buddha image is found inside Wat Chalong's western hall. It is flanked by two statues, one of which supposedly depicts a local man who won several lotteries after praying to the Buddha image *(right)*.

Grand Pagoda

This 197-ft (60-m) tall golden pagoda enshrines a bone splinter of the Buddha. Brought from Sri Lanka in 1999, the fragment is housed inside a *chedi* (stupa) on the third story of the pagoda *(below)*.

Gilded Statues

Cast in bronze, these depictions of former temple abbots are covered in flecks of gold foil. Visitors offer donations and make merit by affixing small pieces of gold-colored foil onto the statues.

Architecture

The temple's colorful multi-tiered sloping roofs, ornate exterior, and interior decorations are very picturesque and provide opportunities for great photographs. The towering golden spire of the Grand Pagoda and glittering window frames are among other visual highlights of Wat Chalong.

Wall Paintings

Inside the Grand Pagoda, wall paintings depict events from the life of Siddhartha Gautama, who became the Buddha after gaining enlightenment. The Buddha is depicted teaching his disciples and receiving offerings, among other acts *(right)*.

Merit-Making

Thai Buddhists visit temples and pay respect to the Buddha, and other spiritual leaders, in order to accumulate merit, with the belief that meritorious deeds will benefit one's position in this life and future lives *(below)*.

Firecrackers

Devotees burst firecrackers to give thanks for answered prayers. The fireworks pop inside a beehive-shaped structure *(below)* located outside, near the sermon hall.

Wax Figures

Lifelike wax models of former temple abbots can be found inside a special exhibition space. Visitors pay tribute to these spiritual leaders to make merit.

Fortune Telling

You can consult the fortune tellers who sit inside the temple's main hall. They shake two cans of numbered bamboo sticks until one stick falls on the floor. The number corresponds to a paper slip inside a wooden cabinet. Retrieve the fortune and ask someone to translate it for you.

Temple History

During an uprising of Chinese tin workers in the late 19th century, many local Thais fled to Wat Chalong for protection. The temple's then abbot, Luang Poh Cham, provided shelter to the people and was later honoured by King Rama V (r. 1868–1910).

Wat Chalong Fair

First held in 1954, the annual Wat Chalong Fair transforms the temple grounds into a bustling entertainment venue featuring live music performances, sermons, and an endless variety of delicious local cuisine. Vendors also set up carnival games, ferris wheels, and merry-go-rounds. The eight-day festival coincides with the Chinese New Year and historically marked the end of a local farm harvest.

⬚⬚ Patong

If you are dreaming of a sleepy tropical hideaway, you might want to look elsewhere – Patong is full of action. The most popular tourist area in Phuket, it features a great range of hotels, restaurants, and nightlife options. Many of the area's high-end resorts are sheltered enclaves with lush gardens and private swimming pools. The seemingly endless shopping options, wild entertainment venues, legendary nightlife, and a host of daytime activities make Patong a favorite destination for people who crave activity on their beach holidays.

Food on display at a roadside stall

🌀 Most prices are negotiable, so be sure to barter with vendors and other service providers.

🔵 Some of the most delicious Thai food is served up at the street-side food carts.

• Map H3
• Patong Boxing Stadium (muay thai fights): 2/59 Sai Nam Yen Road; Map P1; 07634 5185; Adm B1,300 onward; www.boxingstadiumpatong.com
• Bangla Boxing Stadium (muay thai fights): Bangla Road; Map Q1; 07627 3222; Adm B1,300 onward
• Tiger Disco: 49 Bangla Road; 07634 5112
• Banana Disco: 124 Thaweewong Road; 07632 0306
• Seduction Discotheque: 39/1 Bangla Road; 07634 0215; www.seduction-discotheque.com
• Simon Cabaret: Sirirach Road, Patong Beach; 07634 2011; www.phuket-simoncabaret.com

Top 10 Features

1. Patong Beach
2. Water Sports
3. Discos
4. Bangla Road
5. Street Markets
6. Bars
7. Fresh Seafood
8. Massage and Spa Treatments
9. Cabaret Shows
10. Muay Thai Fights

Patong Beach
Phuket's most popular tourist beach teems with sun worshippers – lounge chairs and umbrellas stretch three-deep down the golden-sand beach. Roving vendors sell fresh coconuts, beachwear, and souvenirs. You can also enjoy a massage in the shade.

Water Sports
If you enjoy getting an adrenaline fix at the beach, Patong is the right place for you. From wave running and speedboats to para-sailing and banana boats, Patong Bay offers all the most exhilarating marine activities *(below)*.

Discos
Patong's awesome nightlife needs little introduction. Some of the area's most popular party spots include Tiger Disco, Banana Disco, and Seduction Discotheque. The discos draw in the hordes and dance floors are packed as DJs spin everything from house music to the latest pop favorites *(main image)*.

Bangla Road
The central vein of Patong is ablaze with neon lighting and has music blaring from every direction. There are also numerous open-air bars.

Street Markets
The night markets sell everything from T-shirts to wooden Buddha images, and prices are low. The markets near the beach road offer the widest selection *(above)*.

Bars
As the island's bar capital, Patong boasts a variety of places for enjoying a cold beer or cocktail. From traditional Irish pubs to open-air beer bars, and from go-go bars to sports pubs, Patong has something for everyone.

Fresh Seafood
At sundown, restaurants along the beachfront promenade display the day's fresh catch packed on ice. Snapper, grouper, shrimp, crabs, lobster, and other delicious seafood can be individually selected and grilled and seasoned to your taste *(below)*.

Massage and Spa Treatments
Thailand is renowned for its world-class hospitality, best experienced in its traditional massage treatments and spas. These facilities are ubiquitous in Patong *(left)*.

Cabaret Shows
These colorful shows, starring transvestites, have been thrilling audiences for nearly 20 years. The most popular venue, Simon Cabaret, puts on two shows inside an extravagantly decorated theater.

Muay Thai Fights
No trip to Thailand is complete without watching this Thai martial art *(right)*. Five three-minute rounds, accompanied by romping music, are preceded by the pomp and ceremony of ancient pre-fight rituals.

A Matter of Perspective
Some foreign travelers who arrive in Patong are shocked by the extremely liberal sexual norms of the area, where transsexuals, prostitutes, and occasionally, transsexual prostitutes seem to represent such a large segment of the local population, particularly after the sun goes down. But while seeing the area's "red light" elements is probably unavoidable, it certainly does not mean that Patong only offers such venues. Indeed, there are also plenty of ways to have good, clean fun in Patong.

🔟 Khao Phra Thaeo National Park

Spread across 9 sq miles (23 sq km) of virgin rain forest, this national park in northeast Phuket provides one of the last remaining natural habitats for exotic and endangered animal species on the island. This pristine forest offers a quiet place where visitors can immerse themselves in the jungles that once covered much of the island. Khao Phra Thaeo offers picturesque waterfalls, raw hiking trails, and a rehabilitation center where gibbons receive care and treatment. The park is also home to rare plants, flowers, and trees.

Khao Phra Thaeo National Park headquarters

🕐 **Check the weather forecast before your visit to the park – remember that it can rain without much warning, particularly during the summer months.**

🍴 **Try the Bang Rong Floating Restaurant, not far from Bang Pae Waterfall.**

• Map D5
• Visitor Center: 254 Moo 2, Thepkasattri Road, Thalang; Map D5; 07631 1998; open 8:30am–4:30pm daily; Adm B200 (adults), B100 (children)
• Gibbon Rehabilitation Centre: Bang Pae Waterfall, Pa Khlock, Thalang; Map D5; 07626 0491; open 9am–4:30pm daily; www.gibbonproject.org
• Wildlife Conservation Department and Extension Centre: Highway 4027; Map D5; 07621 1067; open 9am–4pm daily

Top 10 Features

1. Ton Sai Waterfall
2. Gibbon Rehabilitation Project
3. Bang Pae Waterfall
4. Wildlife Conservation Development and Extension Centre
5. Flora
6. Trekking
7. Elephant Trekking
8. Wildlife
9. Virgin Rain Forest
10. Bird-watching

Ton Sai Waterfall

This scenic little waterfall in the center of the wildlife sanctuary is an enjoyable place to spend an afternoon *(above)*. You can climb the rocky paths near the falls, but be careful, since the rocks can get slippery.

Bang Pae Waterfall

The bigger of the national park's two major waterfalls, Bang Pae plummets down and forms a pool ideal for a cool, refreshing dip. The easy walk from the parking lot to the waterfall takes around 10 minutes.

Gibbon Rehabilitation Project

The calls of gibbons resonate through the forest surrounding the Rehabilitation Centre *(above)*, which was established in 1992 to care for animals that had previously been living in captivity. The project reintroduces some gibbons into the wild.

Wildlife Conservation Development and Extension Centre

Located near the base of Ton Sai Waterfall, this visitor center offers lectures on the park's history and purpose, as well as trail guides, brochures, and limited, basic accommodations.

Flora

One of Khao Phra Thaeo National Park's special highlights is a rare and endangered palm known as the white-backed palm, or langkow-palm. Discovered by a German botanist in the 1950s, the fan-shaped plant is unique to southern Thailand.

Trekking

A scenic 5-mile (8-km) long jungle path *(above)* links Ton Sai and Bang Pae waterfalls. Trekkers can hire guides at the visitor center near Ton Sai. Watch out for the park's numerous exotic animal and plant species.

Elephant Trekking

An elephant village on the edge of Khao Phra Thaeo, not far from Bang Pae Waterfall, offers visitors the opportunity to go elephant trekking on jungle trails. The surprisingly nimble animal plods along steadily as you sit high atop its back *(main image)*.

Wildlife

The sanctuary's natural environment is home to a number of exotic species, including wild boar, macaque monkeys, gibbons, and various types of deer.

Virgin Rain Forest

Evergreen trees, bamboo forests, exotic orchids, ferns, and mosses can all be found in Khao Phra Thaeo. The forested area surrounding the sanctuary includes several large rubber tree plantations *(above)*.

Bird-watching

Northern Phuket is a paradise for bird-watchers. Inside the sanctuary, you can spot flowerpeckers, bulbuls, and sunbirds, as well as Green Leafbirds, Red-billed Malkohas, Asian fairy-bluebirds, and brahminy kites *(left)*.

Captive Gibbons

In many of Thailand's tourist areas, local touts carry baby gibbons around and try to lure foreigners into taking photographs with the cute little animals. In exchange, the touts ask for a little money. If you see these touts, remember that the gibbons are being kept illegally, and that many gibbons die when hunters try to capture them for the tourist trade. The Gibbon Rehabilitation Centre at Khao Phra Thaeo National Park works to protect these primates.

🔟 Sirinat National Park

A rugged and pristine beachfront, lined by pine trees, runs along Phuket's northwest coast and marks three largely undeveloped beaches: Mai Khao, Nai Yang, and Nai Thon. Founded in 1981, Sirinat National Park covers an area of 35 sq miles (90 sq km), of which more than three quarters is marine territory. The clean blue waters feature large, healthy coral reefs, and Mai Khao Beach, in particular, has become a well-known sea turtle nesting site. At the northern end of Sirinat is a small, but unspoiled, mangrove forest.

The upmarket JW Marriott Phuket Resort and Spa

🌀 If you cannot afford luxury resorts, pitch a tent on the beach.

🍽 Local seafood restaurants along Route 402 serve excellent fresh fish.

• Map B3
• Visitor Center: 89/1 Moo 1, Baan Nai Yang; Map B3; 07632 7152; open 8:30am–4:30pm daily; www.dnp.go.th/index_eng.asp
• Mai Khao Marine Turtle Foundation; Map B1; 07631 4825; Adm B100; www.maikhaoturtle foundation.com
• Paradise Diving: 116 Moo 5, Sakoo Village, Thalang; Map B4; 07632 8278; Adm B3,290 (Ko Waeo and Tin Mining Wreck); www.dive-paradise.com

Top 10 Features

1. Visitor Center
2. Sea Turtles
3. Mangroves
4. Nature Trail
5. Mai Khao Beach
6. Upmarket Resorts
7. Camping on Nai Yang Beach
8. Nai Thon Beach
9. Snorkeling
10. Scuba Diving

Visitor Center
Located at the southern end of Mai Khao Beach, the Visitor Center provides useful information, including maps. It rents out tents, as well as inexpensive bungalows at the northern end of Nai Yang Beach.

Sea Turtles
Giant sea turtles return to Mai Khao Beach every year between November and March to lay their eggs. The creatures are a fascinating sight. If you spot a turtle on the beach, do not disturb it or touch its eggs.

Mangroves
A mangrove forest can be found at the northern end of Mai Khao Beach. These unique trees, with their tangled roots visible above the shoreline, are crucial in maintaining the ecological balance.

Nature Trail
An elevated walkway *(above)* at the northern end of Mai Khao Beach guides visitors in a circular loop through the mangrove forest, with signs pointing out exotic plant species, including mountain ebony, black myrsina, red cycas, and Lady's Nails quisqualis.

Mai Khao Beach
Phuket's longest beach is a thin, undulating stretch of sand that slopes steeply down into the sea. Lined with magnificent old screw pines, and featuring very little intrusive development, the beach remains one of the island's natural wonders *(above)*.

Nai Thon Beach
This quiet beach north of Bang Tao has managed to retain its sleepy and natural feel despite the development of better road access. Small coral reefs located off either tip of the beach provide great opportunities for snorkeling, and the water is generally calm *(right)*.

Snorkeling
There are enjoyable opportunities for snorkeling near the rocky headlands at both ends of Nai Yang Beach. Vendors rent masks, fins, and snorkels along the beach. Keep your eyes peeled for colorful schools of fish while snorkeling.

Scuba Diving
There is an interesting scuba diving site off the coast of northern Phuket. An old tin dredger that sunk off the coast of Ko Waew is reachable via a short boat ride from Nai Thon Beach. The 164-ft (50-m) long wreck rests at a depth of 53 ft (16 m).

Upmarket Resorts
The beaches of northern Phuket are home to upscale resort properties that harmonize marvellously with the national park surroundings. The JW Marriott, Sala Phuket, and Anantara, among others, offer 5-star luxury amid splendid natural scenery *(see p112)*.

Camping on Nai Yang Beach
Bring your own tent to this beautiful beach *(main image)* or rent one, priced at B225 per night, from the national park's Visitor Center. You can also rent bedding and sleeping mats. The well-kept campgrounds offer toilet and shower facilities.

Turtle Conservation
The Mai Khao Marine Turtle Foundation, along with several Mai Khao Beach resorts, releases dozens of green turtles into the Andaman Sea each year to raise money and awareness for the endangered sea turtles. The conservation effort also includes beach and reef cleaning projects. However, the number of turtles returning to Mai Khao Beach has dwindled; conservationists hope to preserve the area as an annual nesting site.

🔟 Naiharn Beach

Framing an idyllic bay on the island's southwestern tip, Naiharn Beach remains one of Phuket's most pristine waterfronts. The half-mile (1-km) long white-sand beach is flanked by green hills and lapped by turquoise waters. While nearby Naiharn Village has been modernized with cafés, art shops, and guesthouses, the beach and surrounding hills maintain a tranquil, non-commercial vibe, with hotels congregated along only one end. During the high season, a number of private yachts drop anchor in the bay, making Naiharn their temporary home.

Outdoor market at Phromthep Cape

🗝 It is a long distance from Naiharn Village to the beach. Rent a car or motorbike to travel back and forth.

🥥 Drink fresh, cold coconut water on the beach.

• Map H6
• Sinbi Muay Thai: 100/15 Moo 7, Sai Yuan Road, Rawai; Map H5; 083 391 5535; www.sinbi-muaythai.com
• Rawai Supa Muay Thai: 43/42 Moo 7, Soi Sai Yuan, Rawai; Map H5; 0766 8116

Top 10 Features

1 Naiharn Beach
2 Phromthep Cape
3 Surfing
4 Yanui Beach
5 Naiharn Buddhist Monastery
6 Beachside Lunch
7 Ao Sane Beach
8 Muay Thai
9 Windmill Viewpoint
10 Naiharn Lake

Naiharn Beach
Relax under a sun umbrella, catch a tan on the powdery white sand, or wade out into the emerald waters – Naiharn Beach will satisfy even the toughest critic's ideal of a tropical paradise *(main image)*.

Phromthep Cape
The sunsets here are very popular – crowds flock to the beach each evening to witness the multi-colored skies over the Andaman Sea at sundown. Phromthep Cape also boasts a market, restaurant, elephant shrine *(above)*, and lighthouse.

Surfing
The gently tumbling waves and sandy shoreline here attract many boogie-boarders; the few surfers restrict themselves to the southern end of the beach *(below)*.

Yanui Beach
Just south of Naiharn Beach, and accessible via the road that leads to Phromthep Cape, this small V-shaped stretch of sand offers seclusion amid the shade of coconut palms. Yanui Beach also has a small Thai restaurant and a few simple bungalows.

Naiharn Buddhist Monastery
Located behind Naiharn Beach, this spiritual center *(above)*, which owns the beachfront, is said to be partly responsible for keeping the area from getting overdeveloped. The best time to visit is at dawn, when locals make merit by offering food to the monks.

Beachside Lunch
Shaded by a canopy of umbrellas and pine trees, the open-air restaurants at Naiharn Beach serve reasonably priced fresh fruit shakes, sandwiches, and a wide selection of Thai dishes.

Ao Sane Beach
With its rocky shoreline and rough slope down into the sea, Ao Sane Beach *(below)* does not see hordes of swimmers. However, it is a prime spot for snorkelers who claim that the visibility and nearby corals are among the best in Naiharn.

Muay Thai
A number of *muay thai* gyms have been established in Naiharn Village. Visitors can punch some heavy bags, skip rope, and hit the pads with former professional Thai fighters.

Windmill Viewpoint
Perched high on the hills overlooking Naiharn Beach, the Phromthep Alternative Energy Station is the ideal location for capturing the perfect beach photograph.

Explosive Growth
Until just a few of years ago, the beach and village at Naiharn were still a quiet hideaway that not many people knew about. The sleepy village had a few open-air restaurants and guesthouses, but not much more. Later, like the rest of Phuket, a frenzy of development began as resorts, residences, and restaurants started popping up throughout the town. Today, the beach remains one of Phuket's most beautiful, but attracts many more visitors than it did in the past.

Naiharn Lake
Bicyclists and joggers enjoy the paved half-mile (1-km) long route encircling this inland freshwater lake *(above)*. With sea breezes, it also makes for a pleasant picnic destination. Popular cafés and bars can be found on the lake's northwestern shore.

10 Kata Beach

Located just south of Karon, the scenic Kata Beach, comprising two bays separated by a small rocky headland, offers an ideal balance of tropical scenery and well-developed tourism infrastructure. Kata has a number of high-end resorts, making it a popular destination for couples and families. Palm trees fringe the white-sand beach, and the turquoise waters offer good swimming conditions throughout the year. One can even swim to nearby Ko Pu, a small island, passing lovely coral reefs along the way.

Beach bar near
Karon Viewpoint

Top 10 Features

1. Kata Yai
2. Kata Noi
3. Karon Viewpoint
4. Dino Park Mini-Golf
5. Thai Cooking Class
6. Elephant Trekking
7. Spa and Massage Treatments
8. Shopping
9. Nightlife
10. Water Sports

🌅 Karon Viewpoint is an excellent place to watch the sunset.

🍷 Wine lovers can visit the Boathouse Wine and Grill, featuring more than 800 labels.

• Map H5
• Kok Chang Safari: 287 Moo 2, Kata Sai Yuan Road, Kata; Map H4; 084 841 9794; Treks from 8:30am–5:30pm; www.kokchangsafari.com
• Dino Park Mini-Golf: Marina Phuket Resort, Karon Beach; Map H4; 07633 0625; open 10am–midnight daily
• Adm B240 (adult), B180 (children); www.dinopark.com
• Boathouse Wine and Grill: Kata Beach; Map H5; 07633 0015–7; Adm (for cooking class) B2,600; www.boathousephuket.com
• Kata Thai Cooking Class: 5 Ket Kwan Road, Kata Beach; 07628 4510; www.katathaicooking.com

Kata Yai
When people mention Kata, they are usually referring to Kata Yai *(above)*, which is the larger of the two Kata bays, and boasts more resorts and activities. The beach is separated from Kata Noi by a small rocky headland.

Kata Noi
The more secluded Kata beach, located just south of Kata Yai, generally offers more space and privacy than its larger counterpart, especially during the low season.

Karon Viewpoint
Reached via the coastal road south toward Naiharn, this viewpoint provides gorgeous views of the island. Look north and you'll see three white-sand beaches along the coastline *(main image)*.

Dino Park Mini-Golf
With a 39-ft (12-m) high waterfall and an erupting volcano, the setting at this miniature golf course is nothing short of charming. Playing a round is a great way to beat the afternoon heat.

Thai Cooking Class

Learn how to make delicious Thai curries, spicy stir-fries, noodles, and more at any of the numerous popular cooking classes offered in Kata – one is hosted at the upscale Boathouse Wine and Grill restaurant *(left)* and another at the Kata Thai Cooking Class.

Elephant Trekking

Kok Chang Safari Elephant Trekking, not far from Karon Viewpoint, offers rides on the forested hillside. You might even see the amusing sign for "elephant crossing" on the coastal road.

Spa and Massage Treatments

Experience an hour-long traditional Thai massage, available at many venues throughout Kata. Even better, look for the canopy-covered massage beds along the beach.

Shopping

The beach vendors in Kata sell beachwear, coconuts, and snacks, while the off-beach stalls are a shopper's paradise. These outlets sell a wide range of inexpensive clothing and souvenirs *(above)*.

Nightlife

Less wild than Patong, Kata's nightlife nonetheless offers plenty of options for those who wake up when the sun goes down. Most bars are open-air, dotted with festive lights, and play music aimed at pleasing a crowd that wants to relax and chat *(below)*.

Water Sports

The best season for surfing in Kata is from May to October. The waters around Kata are great for beginners since the waves are not too large. If surfing is not for you, rent a kayak from the north end of the beach.

Development

During the 1970s, Kata was known as a low-budget backpacker's destination offering inexpensive beach bungalows and cheap guesthouses. However, when Club Med opened its doors in 1985, the area started turning upscale. Today, Kata mostly caters to well-to-do family travelers. Low-cost rooms can still be found along the inland roads, while most of the beachfront properties have been snapped up by high-end developers.

🔟 Similan Islands National Park

Impossibly soft white-sand beaches and emerald-colored waters set the breathtaking backdrop for this island paradise. Renowned as one of the world's top scuba diving destinations, the underwater world here is stunningly beautiful, populated with magnificent corals, colorful fish, and dramatic rock formations. The nine Similan islands also offer remarkable snorkeling and make for great day trips. Make sure you plan your trip to the Similans with a tour operator based on the mainland – scuba diving equipment is not available on the islands.

Yacht anchored at Donald Duck Bay

🚫 The National Park is closed during the rainy season from May through October, so plan your trip accordingly.

🍴 Food options are limited, so if you have special dietary needs, you should pack some food.

• Map D2 • Adm B200 (for adults) • www.dhp. go.th/index_eng.asp

Top 10 Features

1. Ko Similan
2. Ko Miang
3. Live-aboard Boats
4. Anita's Reef
5. Richelieu Rock
6. Beacon Reef
7. Elephant Head Rock
8. Ko Bon
9. Christmas Point
10. East of Eden

Ko Similan
Home to Donald Duck Bay *(main image)*, named for the rock formation that resembles the cartoon character, Ko Similan has powder-soft, white-sand beaches where you can pitch your tent. The island also has scenic walking trails, so carry sturdy shoes and a camera.

Ko Miang
Home to the National Park Headquarters, the second biggest island in the Similans offers campsites and basic bungalows, including some with air-conditioned rooms. You can rent a large tent here for around B450 a night *(above)*.

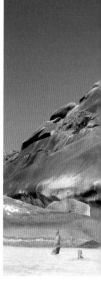

Live-aboard Boats
One of the best ways to experience the dive sites around the Similan Islands is to join a multi-day trip on a live-aboard boat offering several dives each day.

Anita's Reef
This colorful reef spreads across two of the Similan Islands, and is punctuated by large, dramatic boulders. Offering a relatively easy dive, Anita's Reef is often one of the first stops for live-aboard trips.

5 Richelieu Rock

Well known for its exotic marine life, Richelieu Rock became an especially famous diving site ever since whale sharks and manta rays were spotted here *(left)*.

6 Beacon Reef

The longest reef in the Similan Islands, Beacon Reef also marks the place where a live-aboard boat, the *Atlantis X*, sank in 2002. Today, the sunken vessel, resting on a sloping coral wall, is one of the reef's most popular underwater attractions and provides home to a wide variety of marine life.

7 Elephant Head Rock

The largest pinnacle in the Similan Islands juts above the water in a peculiar shape that lends this dive site its name. With its underwater caverns, tunnels, and swim-throughs, this site is home to numerous fish, including small, black-tip reef sharks.

9 Christmas Point

Deep shelves populated by white-tip reef sharks, as well as ribbon eels, make this site popular with divers and underwater photographers *(below)*.

10 East of Eden

A brilliantly colorful reef, East of Eden is one of the most popular dive sites in the Similan Islands. The enchanting reef offers a wide diversity of marine life – teeming with fish, coral, sea fans, and more.

8 Ko Bon

Located in a protected bay and featuring one of Thailand's only vertical dive walls, this site, off Ko Bon, provides marvelous opportunities to see leopard sharks and manta rays *(above)*.

Diving Precautions

Scuba diving is very safe when done correctly, but it can be dangerous – even deadly – for untrained divers. Reputable dive companies require all participants to be PADI (Professional Association of Diving Instructors) certified. A number of companies on Phuket are licensed to provide courses and certification. The beginners' PADI course is called "Open Water Diver" and can be completed in a few days. Visit *www.padi.com* for a list of PADI dive centers in Thailand.

Top 10 Khao Sok National Park

With a land mass encompassing more than 270 sq miles (700 sq km), this national park, located about 110 miles (175 km) north of Phuket, represents southern Thailand's largest virgin forest. Older and more diverse than even the Amazon rain forest, Khao Sok is home to numerous exotic animal and plant species, and has breathtaking natural scenery. Nature lovers will find inspiration in the park's majestic limestone cliffs, rough jungle trails, and placid waterways.

A kite at Khao Sok National Park

🕐 Khao Sok can be visited on a day trip from Phuket, but it is better appreciated with more time.

🍴 Food options are limited inside the park, so bring a packed lunch if you have special needs.

• Map F1; open 9am–4pm daily; Adm B200

• Khao Sok Discovery (jungle trekking and safari tours): 11/36 Moo 5 Chalong; 07652 1857; www.khaosokdiscovery. com

• Paddle Asia (canoeing, kayaking, adventure trips, and jungle trekking): 18/58 Radanusorn; 07624 1519 or 081 893 6558 (cell); www.paddleasia.com

Top 10 Features

1. Sok River
2. Jungle Trekking
3. Elephant Trekking
4. Waterfalls
5. Caves
6. Raft Houses
7. Cheow Laan Lake
8. Wildlife
9. Bamboo Rafting
10. Night Safaris

Sok River
Enjoy a leisurely cruise on a kayak or canoe on this river that meanders through lush jungles and past towering limestone rocks. Along the riverbanks, exotic hornbills, snakes, and long-tail macaque monkeys make their homes. The scenic river offers a relaxing way to experience the park's natural wonders.

Jungle Trekking
Take a walk on the well-beaten paths or follow a guide, who will lead you through the untamed jungle with a machete. The trekking opportunities in the park are second to none, with exceptional caves, lakes, and waterfalls as highlights *(below)*.

Elephant Trekking
The massive, but nimble elephants plod slowly through virgin rain forests while you sit in a special chair atop their backs. Some tours head to natural waterfalls, where you can dismount for a dip in the cool water.

Waterfalls
There are a number of scenic waterfalls in the park, though finding them sometimes requires the assistance of a local guide. Bang Hua Raet, Wang Yao, and Wing Hin waterfalls are located within a 1-mile (2-km) radius of the park headquarters.

Caves
5 Enter the tantalizing darkness of one of the national park's many caves, including the popular Tham Nam Talu and Ha Roi Rai caves. These grottoes have fascinating stalagmites and stalactites *(left)*, and also legions of screeching bats.

Cheow Laan Lake
7 Surrounded by verdant forests and towering mountains, this lake was formed when Ratchaprapha Dam was constructed *(main image)*.

Bamboo Rafting
9 Float down the Sok on a unique watercraft *(below)* fashioned out of lengths of bamboo, taking in the trees, magnificent mountains, and wildlife.

Wildlife
8 A bird-watcher's paradise, the national park has numerous exotic species including hornbills, kingfishers, wild pigs, and eagles. Wildlife enthusiasts can spot Asiatic black bears and much more *(see pp28–9)*.

Night Safaris
10 As some animal species can only be spotted after dark, night river safaris are a popular way to see these unique creatures. Canoes or bamboo rafts are used to quietly glide down the Sok river.

Raft Houses
6 Floating thatched-roof raft houses line the banks of Cheow Laan Lake, allowing visitors to spend a night or longer immersed in the area's tranquil natural surroundings *(above)*. When the sun rises in the morning, dive into the lake for a brisk morning swim or enjoy a canoe ride.

Bua Phut
These gigantic red flowers, whose diameter can reach up to 35 inches (90 cm), are popular with visitors, although finding one in bloom often requires good timing and the assistance of a local guide. Known scientifically as *Rafflesia kerrii*, the flowers are abundant during the winter, from January to March, and have a pungent odor to attract flies for pollination. Be careful around these flowers; the species is endangered.

Left **Clouded leopard resting on a branch** Right **Herd of elephants in the national park**

🔟 Exotic Animal Species in Khao Sok National Park

Bamboo Rat
With short bulky bodies covered in spiky fur, these nocturnal rodents live predominantly in bamboo thickets, as well as in grasslands and forests. Bamboo rats have sharp teeth and claws that are ideally suited to digging the burrows in which they sleep during the day.

Barking deer in the wild

Barking Deer
Also known as muntjac, these small, brown-haired deer have short antlers. They are called barking deer because they are known to bark when they sense danger. Spotting these animals in Khao Sok National Park is quite common.

Malaysian Sun Bear
A small bear that generally weighs less than 143 lb (65 kgs), this threatened species resides in dense forests, where it sleeps and sunbathes in trees. An omnivore, the Malaysian sun bear has no real predators, other than the occasional human.

Cobras
Khao Sok National Park is home to four different species of cobra – monocled cobras, spitting cobras, king cobras, and Asian cobras. The king cobra is the world's longest venomous snake, reaching lengths greater than 16 ft (5 m).

Clouded Leopard
Exceptional climbers, with large feet and powerful claws, clouded leopards have a beautiful yellow-brown coat with distinctive cloud markings. The animal rests and sleeps in trees. Its prey includes small mammals and birds, among other creatures.

Hornbill
The hornbill's long down-curved mandible and distinctive yellow/red horn make the bird easily identifiable. Feeding on fruits, berries, insects, small mammals, and eggs, hornbills often reside in dense forests. Many species can be spotted in Khao Sok National Park.

Hornbill in flight in Khao Sok

Tarantula

These massive spiders tend to dwell inside underground burrows. The species found in Thailand move quickly and are known to be aggressive, so you are advised to give the tarantula plenty of space if you encounter one in the wild.

Tiger

Many of Thailand's 200 to 250 remaining wild tigers are believed to be living in Khao Sok, although you are unlikely to catch a glimpse of one. If you are lucky, however, you might come across tiger tracks.

Malaysian Tapir

With its distinctive proboscis, this large-bodied herbivore looks somewhat like a pig with an elephant's trunk. The tapir's black color provides camouflage so that when it is lying down, the animal looks like a rock.

Grazing Malaysian tapir

Elephant

Wild elephants still roam Khao Sok National Park. Sadly, however, these majestic creatures, the symbol of Thailand, are an endangered species. Herds of elephants can occasionally be spotted in forested areas near watering holes and elsewhere.

Top 10 Flora in the Khao Sok National Park

1. Rain Forest Vegetation
2. Coconut Palms
3. Buttressed Roots Trees
4. Ficus Trees
5. Bamboo Trees
6. Tropical Pitcher Plants
7. Dipterocarps Trees
8. *Rafflesia Kerrii*
9. Banana Trees
10. Liana Vines

History of the Park

Before it was declared a national park in 1980, the forest-covered land known today as Khao Sok was a wilderness that stretched to Myanmar. Few roads bisected this territory, and animal populations, including tigers, flourished. When Ratchaprapha Dam was built in the mid-1980s, numerous trees were chopped down. Poachers also threatened the stability of some animal populations. Today, under the protection of the National Park Service, Khao Sok is home to lots of exotic species, and many poachers have become conservationists.

Visitor Center

Tiger in Khao Sok National Park

🔟 Phang Nga Bay

Dramatic limestone formations jut from this bay, creating a picturesque backdrop for cruises, kayaking excursions, or island-hopping tours. Sights range from movie sets to villages on stilts. Eco-friendly kayaking tours explore sublime lagoons that retain the signs of an earthly Eden, while numerous deserted beaches, tiny island hideaways, and undeveloped tropical lands wait to be discovered in Phang Nga Bay. Meanwhile, Ko Phi Phi enjoys a status worldwide for its natural beauty and for its reputation as a vibrant island party destination.

A kayaker at Loh Dalum Bay

🚣 Hire a longtail boat at Naiharn Beach to visit some of the islands.

🛒 Support the locals – buy food or refreshments if they're selling them.

• Map F2
• King Cruiser Wreck, Sunrise Divers (scuba diving): 269/24 Patak Road, Karon Plaza; 07639 8040; www. sunrise-divers.com
• Spirit of Phang Nga (full-day cruise): 07637 6192; 7:30am–6pm daily; Adm B3,700 onward (adult), B1,850 onward (children); www. asian-oasis.com
• John Gray's Sea Canoe (kayaking): 124 Soi 1 Yaowarat Road, Phuket Town; 07625 4505–7; Daytrips B3,950 onward (adult), B1,975 onward (child); www.johngray-seacanoe.com

Top 10 Features

1. Ko Phi Phi Don
2. Ko Phi Phi Ley
3. Underwater World
4. Phi Phi Viewpoint
5. Khao Khian
6. Ko Yao Noi
7. James Bond Island
8. Ko Panyee
9. Chinese Junk Boat
10. Kayaking

1 Ko Phi Phi Don

With its limestone cliffs and clear waters, this beautiful island is popular for snorkeling and diving. At its heart is Tonsai village, home to most of the hotels, restaurants, and shops. The island also offers quieter resorts on more secluded beaches *(main image)*.

3 Underwater World

A number of popular dive sites, including a sunken passenger ferry between Phuket and Ko Phi Phi, can be found in Phang Nga Bay. You can also snorkel to coral reefs *(left)*.

2 Ko Phi Phi Ley

Home to the stunning Maya Bay, this uninhabited island *(right)* allows overnight visitors to camp on the white sands where Leonardo DiCaprio starred in *The Beach*. Cliff jumping, swimming, and snorkeling are other popular activities here.

Phi Phi Viewpoint
Perched high atop Ko Phi Phi Don, this viewpoint gazes down on two splendid bays, Loh Dalum and Tonsai. From here, visitors get a bird's eye-view of the island's unique dumbbell shape *(above)*.

Khao Khian
Also known as "Writing Hill," this cave in Phang Nga Bay has ancient drawings of humans, birds, fish, and other marine life. The artistry dates back some 3,000 years.

Ko Yao Noi
With unspoiled coastlines, pristine beaches, and thatched-roof bungalows, this island – part of a two-island chain – exudes tranquil vibes.

James Bond Island
The backdrop for 007's infamous duel in *The Man with the Golden Gun*, the island – also known as Ko Khao Phing Kan – today represents one of Phuket's most popular island day trips *(below)*.

Ko Panyee
The village on this island has been constructed on stilts above the shallow waters of the south coast. Most of Ko Panyee's landmass is consumed by a towering limestone rock. The island is one of Phang Nga Bay's most unique attractions.

The "Perfect Beach"
When Hollywood set out to portray the "perfect" tropical island on the silver screen, Maya Bay won the role with its turquoise waters and white sand beach. Released in 2000, *The Beach*, starring Leonardo DiCaprio, makes a compelling case for Ko Phi Phi Ley's claim as the world's best beach. It is subjective, but no other film has done more to inspire the world's dreams of an island hideaway.

Chinese Junk Boat
One of Phuket's classic boat cruises, the Chinese junk-rigged schooner known as *June Bahtra (above)* explores Phang Nga Bay's legendary islands and limestone cliffs, while a separate cruise provides sundown dinner and cocktails.

Kayaking
Paddle through extraordinary aquatic grottoes that open into magnificent open-air lagoons known as *hongs*. These lagoons are populated by exotic birds such as hornbills and kingfishers. The pristine jungle scenery inside the *hongs* is incredible.

Left **Mural of Burmese invaders attacking Phuket** Right **Workers at an opencast tin mine**

🔟 Moments in History

1 1st Century BC–AD 2nd Century: Earliest Records

Phuket was founded by Indian merchants, with trade dating back to the 1st century BC. It was later mentioned by the Greek geographer Ptolemy, who referred to it as "Junk Ceylon," a "cape" en route to the Malaysian peninsula.

2 AD 1500–1700: Tin Seekers

Tin defined Phuket's economy for hundreds of years. The Dutch established a strategic trading presence in Phuket after it was discovered that the island had vast tin reserves. The English and French followed shortly after, and the Siamese King Narai (r.1656–88) granted France monopoly in 1685.

3 AD 1688: French Expulsion

After the Siamese revolution of 1688, in which the pro-foreign Siamese King Narai was overthrown, the French were ordered out of Siam. The French, under General Marshal Desfarges, captured Phuket in an attempt to reassert influence in Siam in 1689, but the occupation of the island was futile.

4 March 13, 1785: Burmese Invasion Repelled

Led by two sisters – Thao Thep Kasattri and Thao Srisoonthorn – the Siamese defended Phuket against a month-long Burmese attack. Francis Light, an English ship captain, had alerted Phuket of assembling Burmese forces, giving the army time to prepare.

5 Early 19th Century

Lured by Phuket's flourishing tin mines, and to escape poverty in their own country, thousands of Chinese workers immigrated to the island during the early 1800s, establishing communities and customs that define Phuket to the present day. Chinese shrines, architecture, and festivals are among the legacies of the era.

Chinese citizens of Phuket in 1942

6 1876: Tin Worker Rampage

A group of migrant Chinese tin workers, disgruntled over their wages and difficult living conditions, instigated a violent uprising on Phuket, causing local residents to flee to Wat Chalong for protection. The temple's monks sheltered the people and eventually helped restore calm to the island.

7 1933: Phuket Province

During the reign of King Rama V (r.1867–1910), Phuket solidified its role as the administrative center of the southern provinces. The island was, however, only a rural subdivision at the time. It became a full province

Preceding pages **Half-buried Buddha, Wat Prathong**

in 1933 after the country shifted from an absolute monarchy to a parliamentary government.

8 1970s: Phuket Discovered
Although the island had been a hotbed of international economic activity for centuries, some still claim that Phuket was discovered by Western backpackers in the 1970s. It is true, however, that the revival in travel during this decade led to the first substantial tourism infrastructure, such as a Club Med resort and regular THAI Airways flights.

9 2000: *The Beach* Filmed
Visitors had been flocking to Thailand's white-sand beaches long before this Hollywood film was made, but there was something about seeing the perfect beach on the silver screen that captured the audiences' imaginations. With global travel on the rise, large numbers of travelers visited Maya Bay *(see p30)*.

10 26 December 2004: Indian Ocean Tsunami
The devastation caused by the tsunami was immense – thousands of lives lost in a matter of minutes. In Thailand, the tsunami represented the worst natural disaster in history, leaving some 8,000 people dead. Busy merchant streets became lethal rapids, and everything on Ko Phi Phi was essentially washed away.

Shops destroyed during the tsunami

Top 10 Historical Figures

1 Rene Charbonneau (17th century)
French medical missionary who served as Phuket's governor.

2 Alexandre Chevalier de Chaumont (1640–1710)
France's first ambassador to Siam, he was granted the country's tin monopoly in 1685.

3 Thao Thep Kasattri (18th century)
This gutsy woman rallied Siamese troops to rebel against the Burmese invasion.

4 Thao Srisoonthorn (18th century)
The Heroines' Monument was built in honor of Thao and her sister *(see above)*.

5 Captain Francis Light (1740–94)
Alerted the administration in 1785 that Burmese troops were massing for an attack.

6 King Rama V (1853–1910)
Credited with modernizing Siam, and preventing the nation from being colonized.

7 Luang Pho Cham (19th century)
Monk who sheltered local residents during a violent tin worker uprising in 1876.

8 Edward Miles (1849–1944)
Australian ship captain who established the first tin dredge in Phuket in 1907.

9 Mom Luang Tri Devakul (20th century)
Hotelier and restaurateur who has helped raise Phuket's luxury standards since the 1980s.

10 Pote Sarasin (1905–2000)
Thai politician after whom the Sarasin Bridge (completed 1967) was named.

Left **Inside Wat Srisoonthorn** Center **Motif, Wat Prathong** Right **Wat Phranang Sang**

Buddhist Temples

Wat Suwan Khiri Khet

Also known as Wat Karon because of its location, this temple features engravings depicting scenes from the Buddha's life on the doors and windows. Two fantastic turquoise *naga* serpents encircle the main temple building and form railings down to the entrance. A smaller building guarded by a yak (mythical character in the Thai *Ramayana*) statue houses an attractive black sapphire Buddha image. ◈ *Patak Road, Karon • Map H4 • Open 8am–5:30pm daily*

Wat Prathong

Built in the 1750s, and known locally as Wat Phra Phut, this colorful temple *(see p83)* is Phuket's second most important after Wat Chalong. The half-buried golden Buddha statue is the main attraction here. According to legend, anyone who attempts to uproot the statue will be cursed.

Wat Phranang Sang

Built more than 200 years ago, Phuket's oldest temple houses the mummified relics of a former abbot, Luang Poh Bai, and a collection of large tin Buddha images, crafted when tin was still considered a semi-precious metal. The Heroines' Monument stands near this temple. ◈ *Thepkasattri Road • Map C5 • Open 8am–5:30pm daily*

Wat Srisoonthorn

Towering above this temple is a massive 95-ft (29-m) tall reclining Buddha statue, depicting the Buddha as he achieved Enlightenment. Nine other Buddha statues populate the entranceway. Built in 1792, and known locally as Wat Lipon, the temple was later renamed Wat Srisoonthorn to commemorate one of the two sisters *(see p35)* who defended Phuket from foreign conquerors. ◈ *Thepkasattri Road • Map C6 • Open 7am–5:30pm daily*

Wat Chalong

Phuket's movisited temple comprises a number of ornately decorated buildings, including a pagoda believed to enshrine a bone fragment of the Buddha. The temple also has statues of former monks, life-like wax models, and displays of fireworks by devotees expressing their gratitude for answered prayers. The annual Wat Chalong Fair is held at the temple around the Chinese New Year *(see pp12–13)*.

The Grand Pagoda, Wat Chalong

Wat Kajonrangsan

A unique temple in Phuket Town, Wat Kajonrangsan, also called Wat Kajon, features distinctive Roman-style architecture in the *ubosot* (ordination chapel). Since it does not draw busloads of tourists, a visit here offers a good opportity to witness an active community environment. The temple grounds also house a school. ◈ *Ranong Road, Phuket Town • Map N5 • Open 7am–5:30pm daily*

Wat Putta Mongkol

Located in the heart of Phuket Town, this temple is sometimes referred to as Wat Klang (literally, central temple). It features colorful architectural designs, including yellow *chedis*, as well as an old Sino-Portuguese colonial home, which is used as the monks' dormitory. The spacious grounds are also home to the Phuket Buddhist Association and Phuket Old Town Foundation. ◈ *Dibuk Road, Phuket Town • Map P5 • Open 8am–5:30pm daily*

Wat Suwan Kuha

This temple is popularly known as Monkey Temple, for the throngs of pesky animals that reside within its grounds begging for, or stealing, food. The actual Buddhist monuments here are located inside a breathtaking cave, with a massive reclining Buddha image forming the centerpiece. Located in Phang Nga, this Buddhist temple is a popular stop for day-trippers from Phuket. ◈ *Phang Nga • Map F2 • Open 8am–5:30pm daily • Adm*

Wat Kathu

Located just outside Patong, this temple offers a peaceful respite from the surrounding frenzy of tourist activity. Its red

Buddha statues inside Wat Kajonrangsan

windows are decorated in gilt-covered reliefs depicting important scenes from the Buddha's life; colored glass and tiles decorate the exterior. ◈ *Moo 4 Baankathu, Kathu • Map H2 • Open 8am–5:30pm daily*

Wat Kosit Wihan

It takes a bit of a climb to reach this temple carved into a hillside, but you will be rewarded with great views of Phuket Town. On the temple grounds stands a large Buddhist cemetery, and a number of small monuments with photographs of the people who were cremated here. ◈ *Highway 402 • Map K2 • Open 8am–5:30pm daily*

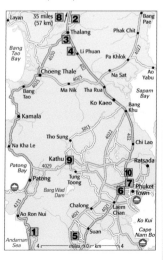

Left **Idols, Bang Niew Shrine** Center **Cherngtalay Shrine** Right **Buddha statues, Kuan Te Kun**

🔟 Chinese Shrines

1 Jui Tui Chinese Temple

This colorful Taoist temple, dedicated to the vegetarian deity Kiu Wong In, plays a central role in the annual Phuket Vegetarian Festival *(see p8)*. Originally built in 1911 on Soi Romanee, the first Jui Tui temple was destroyed by a fire and rebuilt at its current location. ✆ *Soi Phuthorn, Ranong Road, Phuket Town • Map N5 • Open 8am–5:30pm daily*

Relief, Bang Niew Shrine

2 Shrine of the Serene Light

Built by a local Chinese family more than 100 years ago, this historic shrine, once hidden down a narrow alleyway, can be viewed directly from Thalang Road today. Brightly colored ornamentation adorns the roof of the shrine's red-pillared entranceway. ✆ *Chao Fah Nok Road • Map P5 • 07621 1036, 07621 2213 • Open daily*

3 Boon Kaw Kong Shrine

Drivers often honk their car horns for good luck as they pass by this revered shrine located on the hilltop between Patong and Kathu. Besides simply hoping for good fortune, the drivers are also acknowledging the ghosts of travelers who have died while passing over the hill in the past. Well integrated in the local community, this small but popular shrine frequently shows films on a giant outdoor screen. ✆ *Patong Road • Map H2 • Open 9am–5pm daily*

4 Bang Niew Shrine

Destroyed twice by fire, this century-old shrine – also known as Tao Bong Keng or Chai Tueng – plays an important role in the annual Vegetarian Festival. Here, one may see devotees with bizarre piercings, or walking across red-hot coals. The shrine houses deities believed to assist worshippers with their career aspirations. ✆ *Ong Sim Phai Road, Phuket Town • Map Q6 • Open 7am–5:30pm daily*

5 Sam San Shrine

Built in 1853 and dedicated to Mazu, the Chinese goddess of the sea, this shrine frequently hosts ceremonies to consecrate new boats before their maiden sea voyage. The shrine pays homage to the patron saint of sailors, and also features a number of intricate carvings. ✆ *Krabi Road, Phuket Town • Map N5 • Open 8am–5:30pm daily*

Facade of the Sam San Shrine

6 Put Jaw Chinese Temple

The island's oldest Chinese temple is dedicated to the goddess of mercy. Those suffering from health afflictions often come here to pray for relief; the monks here also hand out prescriptions for Chinese herbal medicines. The temple helps parents name their newborn babies. ❧ *Soi Phuthorn, Ranong Road, Phuket Town • Map N5 • Open 6:30am–8pm daily • Adm*

Devotee at Put Jaw Chinese Temple

7 Tha Rua Chinese Shrine

The largest Chinese temple in Phuket, Tha Rua has undergone a series of massive renovations, reported to cost upwards of B40 million and funded entirely by private donations. Colorful, with bold dragon motifs and brilliantly lit at night, the new Tha Rua Chinese Shrine is far more elaborate in scale than its predecessor. ❧ *Thepkasattri Road • Map J1 • Open 6am–6pm daily*

8 Cherngtalay Shrine

Popular with local community members who seek healing from the shrine's deities, Cherngtalay Shrine dates back more than 100 years to the founding of a settlement of Chinese tin-mine workers. The ornately decorated tile roof depicts eight immortal Chinese gods, along with the colorful

dragon imagery common to many of these temples. ❧ *Thalang District • Map B6 • Open 7am–5:30pm daily*

9 Kathu Shrine

Credited as the first Chinese shrine on Phuket to celebrate the Vegetarian Festival, this temple features a fascinating collection of Taoist deity statues in a variety of postures. These intricately designed statues are the main objects of worship at the shrine. ❧ *Kathu Village • Map H2 • Open 8am–5:30pm daily*

10 Kuan Te Kun Shrine

Though less prominent than some of the other shrines on Phuket, Kuan Te Kun – commonly known as Sapam Shrine – nonetheless served as the opening location for the island's massive nine-day Vegetarian Festival in 2010. With brilliantly colored dragons encircling its four main pillars, and others guarding its entrance, Kuan Te Kun is full of photographic opportunities. ❧ *Sapam Village • Map K1 • Open 8am–5:30pm daily*

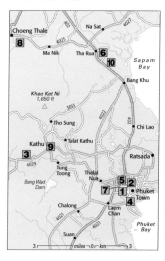

Left **Sun umbrellas on Naiharn Beach** Right **Jet-skis on Patong Beach**

🔟 Beaches

1 Patong Beach
More a tropical playground than a hideaway, Patong is the epicenter of activity on Phuket, and its beach is no exception. With rows of lounge chairs and sun umbrellas stretching down the entire length of sand, Patong Beach is a bustling extension of the town. Jet-skis, parasailing, banana boats, and vendors of every kind all vie for attention *(see p14)*.

2 Kata Beach
The seashore here has two separate beaches, Kata Yai and Kata Noi, which are divided by a rocky cliff. Kata Yai is the larger, and busier, of the two. Once a haven for backpackers and hippies, Kata Beach today caters to an increasingly upscale crowd, and is very popular for its stunning beauty *(see pp22–3)*.

3 Karon Beach
This large beach offers plenty of space for sunbathers who want a little privacy. With

Breathtaking view of Karon Beach

more than 3 miles (5 km) of powdery white sand lapped by the turquoise waters of the Andaman Sea, Karon Beach is often less crowded than its busier neighbors in Patong and Kata. The magnificent coral reef at its southern end is perfect for snorkeling. ◈ *Map H4*

4 Long Beach
With some of the best beach-access snorkeling on Ko Phi Phi and with breathtaking views of Ko Phi Phi Ley, Long Beach is both secluded and scenic. During the afternoon, it caters almost exclusively to travelers here; nights are blissfully quiet. ◈ *Map M6*

5 Maya Bay
Perhaps the world's most famous beach after its role in the Hollywood blockbuster *The Beach,* starring Leonardo DiCaprio, the beautiful Maya Bay on Ko Phi Phi Ley has almost single-handedly inspired travelers worldwide to visit southern Thailand. With its sparkling turquoise waters and exquisite white sand – not to mention the near total absence of development – perhaps Maya Bay truly is paradise *(see p30)*.

6 Bang Tao Beach
Home to annual international windsurfing competitions, Bang Tao is one of Phuket's best places to catch a wave. The

upscale Laguna Phuket Resort complex occupies the middle of the beach, while the northern end is undeveloped, offering a respite from the crowds. You can ride horses – or better yet, elephants – on the soft golden sand here. ◈ Map B5

Rows of lounge chairs and sun umbrellas, Bang Tao Beach

Surin Beach

Populated by numerous high-end resorts, and with expensive private homes on the surrounding hillside, Surin Beach is sometimes referred to as Millionaire's Row. The beach is very popular with locals, who appreciate the area's excellent seafood. The water is calm and clear from November to April, but be cautious about undertows during the low season. ◈ Map A6

Naiharn Beach

A quiet beach on Phuket's southwestern tip, Naiharn is framed by rolling green hills and emerald waters, and offers a perfect hideaway far from the crowds. The calm, warm water is ideal for swimming, and because there is just one resort property here – the unimposing Royal Phuket Yacht Club Hotel (see p113) – travelers feel as if they've stumbled upon a well-kept secret (see pp22–3).

Mai Khao Beach

Protected as part of Sirinat National Park, Mai Khao Beach does not look like a standard Phuket tourist beach. The undulating sand, lined with wonderful old screw pines, slopes down to the sea. There are no private watercraft and most of the buildings along Mai Khao are luxury resorts, none of which infringe on the area's natural beauty (see p19).

Loh Dalum Beach

This picture-postcard beach, outlined by green hills and craggy cliffs, is understandably one of Ko Phi Phi's most popular destinations. Swimmers can wade into its turquoise waters, which, even at a distance from the shore, are only waist deep. In the distance, the colored cliffs of Nui Bay rise up like paintings on the sky. ◈ Map L6

Left **View of Loh Dalum Bay from Phi Phi Viewpoint** Right **Entrance to the Karon Viewpoint**

Viewpoints

Karon Viewpoint
With breathtaking views of Kata Noi, Kata, and Karon beaches, this famous viewpoint in the rolling hills of southwestern Phuket is a great stopover for travelers headed south to Naiharn Beach or Phromthep Cape. Called *khao saam haad* in Thai (literally, hill of three beaches), Karon Viewpoint has well-tended gardens and a sheltered viewing pavilion *(see p22).*

Phromthep Cape
At sundown, all eyes face west from this magnificent perch on Phuket's southernmost tip *(see p20).* Romantic and awe-inspiring, the multi-colored sunsets here attract visitors from all over Phuket. Kaew Yai Island can be seen off the coast, and you can see as far as Ko Phi Phi from the Phromthep Cape

Khao Khad Views Tower

lighthouse. The atmospheric Phromthep Restaurant overlooks Naiharn Beach.

Windmill Viewpoint
This energy station atop Phuket's southern hills overlooks Naiharn Beach and provides an opportunity to capture magnificent panoramic photographs of the entire length of white sand. Home to the Phromthep Alternative Energy Station, Windmill Viewpoint is less crowded than Phromthep Cape, and both sights can easily be visited on the same day. Map H6

Big Buddha Viewpoint
With sweeping 360-degree views of Phuket, this religious site, home to a massive cross-legged Buddha image, is located 1,312 ft (400 m) above sea level. Tinkling bells line the pathway leading to the marble Buddha statue. Dress conservatively to respect the Buddha's spiritual significance. The restaurant here provides fantastic views. Map H4 • Open 8am–7:30pm daily

Khao Khad Views Tower
This hilltop tower in Cape Panwa has picturesque views of southern Phuket, including the Big Buddha statue atop a distant hill. Also known as Panwa Viewpoint, Khao Khad Views Tower has two levels. Visitors are provided with photo maps describing the various sights in the distance. Map K4

Rang Hill

A popular hangout for local students, romantic couples, and others, this peaceful hilltop oasis above Phuket Town offers refreshing breezes and plenty of greenery, providing an ideal setting for anyone who wants to

Visitors enjoying views of Phuket Town from Rang Hill

exercise, enjoy a picnic, or read a book. Leafy trees provide lots of shade, while the two restaurants provide marvelous views of Phuket Town (see p9).

Monkey Hill

Visitors will not be surprised, given this hill's name, when they encounter macaque monkeys on the way up this hill. A television station prevents climbers from reaching the hill's actual summit, but one will find many worthwhile views of the ocean and city through the trees on the hillside (see p9).

Radar Hill Viewpoint

Some 1,640 ft (500 m) above sea level, the tallest point on Phuket is home to a weather station whose domed roof can be clearly seen from the beaches below. Steep roads wind up toward the summit but stop just short of the entrance to the military-controlled buildings. The drive affords several staggering views of Phuket. Map H3

Phi Phi Viewpoint

A delightful destination for watching the sunrise or sunset, this viewpoint on Ko Phi Phi Don requires a 30-minute stroll. At a height of 610 ft (186 m), it isn't the top of the world, but the views of Tonsai and Loh Dalum

bays, and of Ko Phi Phi Ley, are breathtaking. Signs pointing the way can be found in Loh Dalum Bay. Map M5

Helicopter Charters

For the most thrilling views of the island, and stunning photo opportunities, helicopter tours offer a breathtaking way to see Phuket from above. A number of private flight companies offer chartered sky tours over Phuket's brilliant white-sand beaches, emerald waters, and mangrove coasts, as well as Phang Nga's majestic limestone cliffs. A 10-minute flight costs around B5,000. Adm
• www.skydance.aero

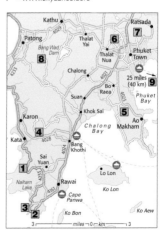

Left **Viking Cave, Ko Phi Phi Ley** Center **Market, Phromthep Cape** Right **Cheow Laan Lake**

🔟 Picturesque Places

Ko Phi Phi Ley

With dramatic limestone cliffs giving way to powdery white sand and crystal-blue lagoons, this uninhabited island is a tropical paradise. Daytrippers enjoy snorkeling and swimming in the placid blue waters surrounding the island, as well as seeing the 400-year-old wall paintings rendered by fishermen in the Viking Cave. You can also spend a night camping on the famous Maya Bay *(see p30)*.

Bang Pae Waterfall

At a height of 59 ft (18 m), this isn't exactly a breathtaking plummet of rushing water, but Bang Pae Waterfall offers a picturesque backdrop for swimming. Located in the jungles of Khao Phra Thaeo National Park, the waterfall is close to the Gibbon Rehabilitation Centre. It's best visited during the rainy season between June and November *(see p16)*.

Khao Rang Viewpoint

With sweeping views of Phuket Town and wide expanses of green ideal for picnics, the top of Rang Hill is one of Phuket's most relaxing places to spend an afternoon. People come here to exercise or read a book. Others enjoy the restaurants with magnificent views and the island's best iced coffee. The bronze statue of a former Phuket governor stands near the viewpoint *(see p9)*.

Phang Nga Bay

Verdant limestone cliffs jut up from this bay, creating a dramatic backdrop with excellent photo opportunities. James Bond Island features one of the most popular of these majestic rock formations. But since it often gets crowded, look for full-day sea canoe journeys through less crowded aquatic grottoes and cavernous tunnels *(see pp30–31)*.

Khao Sok National Park

Beautiful lakes, thrilling caves, and limestone cliffs are interspersed with ancient evergreen trees in this virgin forest north of Phuket. Home to a diverse population of wildlife, as well as rare tree species, Khao Sok offers some of the best trekking, canoeing, and safaris in southern Thailand *(see pp26–9)*.

Trekker in Khao Sok National Park

Phromthep Cape

Dramatic, swirling shades of red, purple, and orange appear on the horizon during the sunset crescendo at Phromthep Cape *(see p20)*. The hilltop viewpoint also has restaurants, an outdoor market, an elephant shrine, and a lighthouse.

Kayaking in the mangrove forests

Mangroves

These fantastic trees, with their tangled and exposed roots, can be found along Phuket's muddy shorelines. Sea canoe tours offer the best way to see the mangroves up close. Above ground, the trees provide homes to crab-eating macaque monkeys, while underwater they serve as nurseries for crustaceans and fish. The trees themselves are picturesque – and somewhat mystifying, because they survive in salt water.

Similan Islands

One of the top scuba diving destinations in the world, the Similan Islands *(see pp24–5)* are home to a variety of colorful and rare marine life, including magnificent coral reefs. Above water, the sight is just as spectacular, with unspoiled, unpopulated beaches. Overnight snorkeling or diving trips allow visitors to sleep in tents, or very basic bungalows, on the beach.

Sirinat National Park

Located in northwest Phuket, Sirinat National Park *(see pp18–9)* protects some of Phuket's last mangroves, as well as a number of pristine beaches, including Mai Khao Beach – home to nesting sites for sea turtles. An elevated nature trail guides visitors through the mangrove forests, with signs explaining the various species.

Cheow Laan Lake

Framed on all sides by tree-covered limestone cliffs, this stunning natural lake in the heart of Khao Sok National Park is populated by floating bamboo raft houses and serves as an ideal venue for swimming and kayaking. In the early morning, the lake's long-tail boats and mist-shrouded shores provide excellent material for photographers. Monkeys, wild boars, and gibbons populate the surrounding forest *(see p27)*.

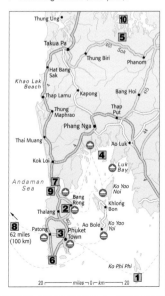

Left THAI Airways Office, Phuket Town Right Flora around Ton Sai Waterfall, Khao Phra Thaeo

TOP 10 Scenic Walks

1 Historical Architecture in Phuket Town

Take a walk back in time past marvelous classic homes and shops built during Phuket's tin boom in the late 19th and early 20th centuries. Many of these houses were constructed in the Sino-Portuguese architectural style. The best routes to take are down Phang Nga, Thalang, Dibuk, Krabi, and Yaowarat roads. Keep an eye out for the spectacular Soi Romanee, located off Thalang Road (see pp10–11).

2 Chinese Shrines in Phuket Town

Another popular way to enjoy the sights of Phuket Town is to focus on its wonderful markets and colorful Chinese shrines. Jui Tui and Put Jaw, two of Phuket's most important Chinese shrines, are located near Ranong Road.

Outside the Put Jaw Shrine, Phuket Town

This walking tour is marked on the Phuket Town Historical Map, distributed free at Phuket International Airport.

3 Khao Phra Thaeo Wildlife Sanctuary

The most popular trek in this national park begins at the park headquarters at Ton Sai Waterfall, navigates through 4 miles (6 km) of virgin forest, and ends at Bang Pae Waterfall. Besides abundant natural plant species, the park is also home to monkeys, flying foxes, wild pigs, and cobras (see pp16–17).

4 Mangrove Forests on Mai Khao Beach

At the northern end of Mai Khao Beach (see p19) stands one of Phuket's most pristine mangrove forests. An elevated walkway guides visitors above these fascinating trees, which survive in saltwater. Signs describe the unusual plant species here, which include black myrsina, red cycas, and mountain ebony.

5 Naiharn Beach to Phromthep Cape

Walk away from the beach, head clockwise around Naiharn Lake, and follow signs to Phromthep Cape. The hilly, stretching walk will take you past Yanui Beach. At the end of the path are two awesome viewpoints – one facing Naiharn Beach (see pp20–21), and the other, westward over the Andaman Sea.

6 Surin Beach to Kamala

From ritzy Surin Beach, home to top-end resort properties, walk south along the sand until you reach a pathway crossing over to Laem Singh Beach. This stunningly pictur-esque cape on the west coast is tucked

Bathing at the upmarket Surin Beach

between Surin and Kamala. Spend some time here before continuing to Kamala, which features a relaxed beach and fishing village.

7 Khao Sok National Park

Trek through ancient forest in Khao Sok (see pp26–9), encoun-tering exotic birds, wildlife, and orchids. Bird-watchers will be delighted to see several species of hornbill, while long-tail macaque monkeys and gibbons swing through the trees above. Paddle Asia offers a popular soft adven-ture tour for spotting wildlife, as well as tailored trips. ✆ Paddle Asia; 07624 1519 or 081 893 6558 (cell); www.paddleasia.com

8 Patong

Begin this stroll from the southern end of Patong Beach around dusk (see p14). As you walk up the main beach road, you'll pass bustling open-air restaurants displaying the day's catch on ice, and lively cocktail-sipping crowds. Turn right onto hedonistic Bangla Road and spend some time people-watching.

9 Similan Islands

Best known for its exciting underwater sites, the Similan Islands (see pp24–5) also offer a few hiking trails. On Ko Similan, the main island, a tree-lined path winds up to a viewpoint with

breathtaking vistas. The best part, of course, is that you'll see hardly a soul on your way up.

10 Khao Lak

A number of hiking trails can be found in and around Khao Lak, including a popular scenic forest path starting near the base of the 33-ft (10-m) tall Chong Fah Waterfall. Sturdy shoes help while walking on the rough jungle trails here. In the past, Buddhist monks maintained forest retreats in the area; the ruins of these shelters can still be seen. ✆ Map E2

Left **Incense for sale during the Chinese New Year** Right **Water fights during Songkran**

🔟 Fairs and Festivals

1 Chinese New Year

Celebrated with firecrackers, crashing cymbals, and colorful costumes, the Chinese New Year marks the beginning of a new lunar year, and is an auspicious day for the Chinese. The holiday is especially important in Phuket Town, where people dress in bright red costumes and numerous parades and feasts are held. 🚫 *Late Jan/early Feb*

Decorations for the Chinese New Year

2 Old Phuket Festival

Chinese opera, rickshaw rides, and a Phuket Baba Light Show are a few of the highlights of Old Phuket Festival, which coincides with the Chinese New Year. The festival is held in Phuket Town on Thalang, Krabi, and Phuket roads. 🚫 *Late Jan/early Feb*

3 Phuket Gay Pride Festival

More than a decade old, this festival includes four nights of wild parties and parades in Patong. With cabaret shows, fashion shows, and more, this annual event seeks to create a stronger gay, lesbian, bisexual, and transgender community on Phuket. 🚫 *Feb*

4 Phuket International Blues Festival

Since its debut in 2005, this popular music festival has grown bigger every year. In 2011, guitar legends such as Mason Ruffner and Curtis Salgado headlined the event. Bands travel from around the globe to play here. 🚫 *25–26 Feb • www.phuketbluesfestival.com*

5 Songkran

The traditional Thai New Year celebration turns the entire country into one big water fight. Getting sprayed with water is considered good luck, and many Thais visit temples to pay respect to Buddha by sprinkling water on his statue. 🚫 *13–15 Apr*

6 Visakha Puja

Thailand's Buddhist temples overflow with merit-makers on this holy day marking the birth, enlightenment, and death of the Buddha – three events that occurred on the same day in different years. At night, believers walk around the temples in a candlelit procession. 🚫 *May*

7 Por Tor Festival

During the annual "Hungry Ghosts" festival, offerings of special cakes, candles, and flowers are made to deceased ancestors, who are believed to revisit their earthly homes on this day. Chinese shrines serve as the center of the festival. ◈ *Aug*

Phuket Vegetarian Festival
Celebrated over nine days, this festival serves to "purify" participants and bring them good health. At many Chinese shrines in Phuket Town, participants invoke the gods by walking on fire, as well as displaying extreme acts of body piercing and self-mortification. ◈ *Late Sept/early Oct • www.phuketvegetarian.com*

Firewalkers at the Phuket Vegetarian Festival

Loy Krathong
Sins of the previous year float away as Thais pay homage to the guardian spirit of water. Participants build small banana-leaf vessels and decorate them with flowers and candles. If a person's boat floats, they will enjoy good luck for the year. ◈ *Late Oct/early Nov*

Chao Ley Boat Floating Festival
At this festival, participants float ceremonial vessels hoping to receive happiness and prosperity, and ward off bad luck. Held in Chao Ley (sea gypsy) villages, the festival also pays tribute to the Chao Ley's ancestors. ◈ *Nov*

Top 10 Sporting Events

1 Muay Thai
No visit to Thailand is complete without witnessing this martial art form. ◈ *Weekly*

2 The Bay Regatta
More relaxed than the King's Cup Regatta, these races are popular with visitors. ◈ *Feb*

3 Phuket Bike Week
An annual gathering of motorcycle enthusiasts, this fest involves music, parties, and awesome bikes. ◈ *Apr*

4 Phuket International Cricket Sixes Tournament
A popular event, this brings international cricketers into competition in Karon. ◈ *Apr*

5 Phuket International Rugby Tournament
This three-day tournament draws teams from Australia and Asia. ◈ *May*

6 Laguna Phuket International Marathon
Runners from around the world compete in this race that starts at Bang Tao Beach. ◈ *Jun*

7 Six Senses Phuket Raceweek
A week of parties and yacht races, this festival attracts many participants. ◈ *Jul*

8 Phuket Surfing Contest
Held at Kata Beach, this contest lets surfers vie for more than B100,000 in prizes. ◈ *Sept*

9 Laguna Phuket Triathalon
This athletic event features a 1-mile (2-km) swim, 34-mile (55-km) cycle race and 8 mile (12-km) run. ◈ *Nov*

10 King's Cup Regatta
The regatta started in 1987, when King Adulyadej celebrated his 60th birthday. ◈ *Dec*

Left **Exhibit at Phuket Cultural Centre** Center **Display at Phuket Seashell Museum** Right **Big Buddha**

🔟 Museums and Monuments

1 Phuket Cultural Centre

This center has a collection of old artifacts that helps tell the cultural history of Phuket and southern Thailand. Visitors might want to request a guide, since most of the information is in Thai *(see p8)*.

2 Kathu Mining Museum

Paying tribute to Phuket's rich tin mining heritage, this museum has dioramas of early mining techniques, caves, and workers in action. Other exhibits show tin dredging operations and a model of an opium den. ◎ *Kathu-Ko Kaeo Road, Kathu district • Map J2 • Open 8am–4pm Mon–Sat • Adm*

3 Heroines' Monument

Unveiled in 1967, this monument depicts the sisters who stalled a Burmese invasion

The Heroines' Monument, Phuket

in 1785 by sending women dressed in army uniforms into the field *(see p34)*. The Burmese forces, thought that these were reinforcements from Bangkok, and withdrew. ◎ *Thepkasatri Road, north of Phuket Town • Map C6*

Traditional clothing

4 Phuket Thai Hua Museum

Originally built as a Thai-Chinese school, this 100-year-old structure *(see p10)* today serves as a museum, exhibition space, and function hall. Visitors can walk through the schoolhouse, which has old photographs and vintage books on display.

5 Phuket Philatelic Museum

Dedicated to Thailand's post office, this museum is housed in an 80-year-old building in Phuket Town. Old telephones, scales, teletype machines, and stamps can be seen here, along with displays on the history of the Thai post office since its beginnings under King Rama V. ◎ *Montri Road, Phuket Town • Map P5 • 07621 1020 • Open 8:30am–4:30pm Mon–Fri, 9am–noon Sat*

6 Phuket Seashell Museum

Housing a private collection, the Phuket Seashell Museum has more than 2,000 varieties of seashells, including a 550-lb (250-kg) exhibit, as well as the world's largest golden pearl. ◎ *12/2 Moo 2, Viset Road, Rawai • Map H5 • 07661 3666 • Open 8am–6pm daily • Adm • www.phuketseashell.com*

7 Thalang National Museum

Phuket's national museum *(see p85)* has displays on the Battle of Thalang, tin mining, sea gypsies, and the history of the Chinese on Phuket. A magnificent 9th-century Vishnu statue, discovered in the 20th century, stands in the main hall.

8 Saphan Hin Mining Monument

Located in a waterfront park, this monument is dedicated to Edward Miles, the Australian ship captain who brought the first tin dredgers to Phuket in 1909. ⓢ *Near Phuket Town, Phuket Road • Map K3*

Saphan Hin Mining Monument

9 Big Buddha

This 148-ft (45-m) tall Buddha *(see p42)* sits high atop Nakkerd Hill, with sweeping views stretching from Chalong Bay to the Andaman Sea. Carved from white Burmese marble, the Buddha sits cross-legged on a podium decorated with lotus flowers.

10 Thavorn Lobby Hotel Museum

In this magnificent wood-panelled hotel lobby, visitors will find a fascinating collection of vintage photographs of old Phuket Town and Thai royalty, classic Thai movie posters, opium pipes, tin mining equipment, and traditional Chinese wedding hats. ⓢ *74 Rassada Road, Phuket Town • Map P5 • 07621 1333–5*

Top 10 Films Shot on Phuket

1 ***The Man with the Golden Gun* (1974)**
This 007 movie featured Ko Khao Phing Kan *(see p31)*, now known as James Bond Island.

2 ***The Killing Fields* (1984)**
Based on the Khmer Rouge regime in Cambodia, this movie shows the French and US embassies in Phuket Town.

3 ***Good Morning, Vietnam* (1989)**
Starring Robin Williams and Jintara Sukapat, this film had jungle scenes shot on Phuket.

4 ***Casualties of War* (1989)**
Brian de Palma's Vietnam War film has realistic jungle scenes filmed on Phuket.

5 ***Heaven and Earth* (1993)**
Chinpracha House *(see p10)* in Phuket Town was featured in this Vietnam War movie.

6 ***Cutthroat Island* (1995)**
Starring Geena Davis, this pirate film was shot in Maya Bay on Ko Phi Phi *(see p30)*.

7 ***Tomorrow Never Dies* (1997)**
Phang Nga Bay *(see p30–31)* was portrayed as Vietnam's Halong Bay in this 007 film.

8 ***The Beach* (2000)**
Ko Phi Phi Ley's Maya Bay stole the show in this movie by Danny Boyle.

9 ***Bridget Jones: The Edge of Reason* (2004)**
Seascapes were filmed near Ko Panyee, and Phuket's airport also received screen time.

10 ***Star Wars: Episode III Revenge of the Sith* (2005)**
Backdrops from just outside of Phuket, in Krabi province, were featured in this movie.

Left **Stylish interior of Baan Rim Pa** Right **Building that houses La Trattoria**

🔟 Restaurants

1 La Trattoria
This award-winning Italian restaurant at Dusit Thani Laguna Phuket *(see p112)* serves authentic homemade pastas as well as other culinary creations. ◎ *390 Srisoonthorn Road, Cherngtalay • Map B6 • 07636 2999 • Open 6:30–10pm daily • www.dusit.com • BBBB*

2 Baan Rim Pa
Perched on a cliff above Kalim and Patong bays, Baan Rim Pa serves royal Thai cuisine, once found only in the kingdom's palaces. ◎ *223 Prabaramee Road, Patong • Map H2 • 07634 0789 • Open 1–11pm daily • BBBB*

3 Joe's Downstairs
With picturesque views of Kalim Bay, this popular spot for sunset cocktails serves Maine lobster, Japanese beef, and Australian short ribs. ◎ *223/3 Prabaramee Road, Patong • Map H2 • 07661 8245 • Open 12:30–11pm daily • BBBB*

4 Sala Bua
Located at Impiana Cabana Resort *(see p113)*, this beachfront restaurant features Thai and Pacific-Rim fusion cuisine. The Australian fire-roasted Chateaubriand is recommended. ◎ *Patong Beach • Map N1 • 07634 0138 • Open 6am–midnight daily • www.sala-bua.com • BBBB*

5 White Box Restaurant
Once a private residence, this Mediterranean- and Thai-inspired eatery has a rooftop lounge with stunning views of Patong Bay, making it popular for cocktails and tapas. In-house jazz musicians and global DJs entertain diners. ◎ *245/7 Prabaramee Road, Patong • Map H2 • 07634 6271 • Open 5pm–1am daily • BBBB*

6 On the Rock
Meals are served on the scenic deck at this renowned seafood restaurant. Getting a beachfront table often requires a reservation. ◎ *47 Karon Road, Karon Beach • Map H4 • 07633 0625 • Open noon–10pm daily • BBBB*

7 Kra Jok See
Tucked into a small 18th-century Sino-Portuguese shop house in Phuket Town, this charming restaurant with exposed wooden beams and candlelit

Popular seaside restaurant, Joe's Downstairs

 Preceding pages **Kayaking, Phang Nga Bay**

ables serves delicious traditional Thai cuisine. But the night really begins after dessert, when the music is cranked up for one of Kra Jok See's legendary dance parties. Reservations are recommended (see p80).

8 Boathouse Wine and Grill

This stylish seaside restaurant features a huge wine cellar with more than 800 labels. The excellent French and Thai degustation menus compete with classic wine and grill favorites, such as prime meat and chops (see p81).

Bar at Boathouse Wine and Grill

9 Silk

A stylish Thai restaurant with contemporary interiors, Silk serves local seafood dishes such as white snapper with ginger, celery, and pickled plums, as well as khao soi (Thai chicken curry with noodles). ⬦ Andara Resort & Villas, Kamala Beach • Map G1 • 07633 8777 • Open 7am–10pm daily • www.andaraphuket.com • BBBB

10 Kopitiam by Wilai

Serving hokkien mee (Hokkien fried noodles), a Phuket specialty, this colorful eatery is the younger sibling of the perinnially popular Wilai restaurant. The space has been designed like a Chinese shop house. Other specialties include phat thai and southern Thai curries (see p80).

Top 10 Thai Dishes

1 Tom Yum Gung
Simmered in a clear broth, this hot and sour prawn soup introduces a world of exhilarating new flavors.

2 Phat Thai
An iconic Thai street food, this features stir-fried rice noodles, eggs, fish sauce, tamarind juice, and more.

3 Phat Kraprao
This spicy, flavorful stir-fry is made with chili and basil leaves and is often served with rice and a fried egg.

4 Gaeng Kiaw Wan
A Thai green curry, this is usually cooked with chicken or beef and can be spicy and a little sweet.

5 Gai Phat Met Mamuang
Chicken stir-fried with cashew nuts is a popular Thai dish, especially in tourist areas.

6 Somtam
A spicy salad made from shredded unripened papaya, Somtam is often eaten with sticky rice.

7 Tom Kha Gai
Made with coconut milk, galangal, lemongrass, and chicken, this is a delicious hot soup.

8 Khao Phat
A simple dish made of Thai fried rice, Khao Phat is often served with cucumber and sweet chili sauce.

9 Por Pia
These Thai spring rolls, usually fried, are often stuffed with vegetables, noodles, and pork or shrimp.

10 Khao Niaw Mamuang
Made with succulent fresh mango and sticky rice, this dish is drizzled with a sweet coconut cream sauce.

For more places to eat on Phuket See pp80–81

Left **A go-go bar signboard** Center **Revellers, Aussie Bar** Right **Cocktail, After Beach Bar**

TOP 10 Bars and Nightclubs

1 Kangaroo Bar
Centrally located on Bangla Road and flanked by about a half-dozen other establishments of a similar vintage, Kangaroo Bar draws lively crowds. This popular venue has an in-house DJ, and is also renowned as a prime vantage point for scoping out Patong's colorful passersby *(see p79)*.

2 Timber Rock
Phuket Town's top live music venue features an excellent in-house band. Busy during the week, and sometimes downright wild on weekends, this is a great place to dance and party. A favorite with local Thais, the bar also attracts its fair share of foreign visitors *(see p79)*.

3 Yoonique Stone Music Café
A local favorite, this funky little dive tucked behind Naiharn Lake in southern Phuket hosts regular jam sessions and live bands in a unique and artistically decorated environment *(see p79)*.

The bar at Yoonique Stone Music Café

4 Aussie Bar
Located right in the middle of Bangla Road, Patong's best-known family-friendly sports bar screens all the big football, cricket, and rugby matches on more than 30 TVs. The bar promotes upcoming games on its website *(see p79)*.

5 Velvet Dojo
Swanky for an island bar, the Velvet Dojo features a stylish lounge that caters to a trendy crowd and upscale travelers who want to chill out. Located in the centre of Tonsai village, and opening on to one of its busiest streets, the bar is hard to miss. The house music and nighttime specials are very good *(see p98)*.

6 Apache Beach Bar
This multi-level nightclub is often packed with people dancing into the early hours. Apache flaunts its flirtatious side with tropical bikini parties, ladies' specials, and body painting parties. The bar also hosts weekly ladyboy shows *(see p98)*.

7 After Beach Bar
Located near Karon Viewpoint, on the winding mountain highway between Kata and Rawai, this relaxing bar overlooking the sea plays a constant stream of reggae and acoustic tunes. It is a popular place for post-beach cocktails while watching the sunset *(see p79)*.

 Patong has many go-go bars (see p59) – venues known for their scantily clad dancers – though they are not to everyone's taste.

Rolling Stoned Bar

8 This popular live music spot on Ko Phi Phi is an ideal place to sprawl out on a floor cushion and listen to cover bands playing your favorite classic and modern rock tunes. The bar's funky lighting and surroundings, as well as its pool tables, have helped Rolling Stoned Bar remain a long-time beach favorite *(see p98)*.

Entrance to the Banana Disco

Banana Disco

9 A long-term crowd pleaser, Banana Disco comes to life around midnight, when crowds flock on to the dance floor to enjoy house music. A great place to dance, flirt, and drink, the disco remains one of Patong's most popular late-night venues. The B200 cover charge gets you one drink *(see p79)*.

Molly Malone's

10 The island's most popular Irish pub has been going strong since it first opened in 1999. Located on the main beach road, Molly Malone's offers live pub-rock each night while a number of flatscreen TVs broadcast live sports events. The lively bar also serves a range of traditional pub fare, as well as brews such as Guinness, Kilkenny, and Magners Irish Cider on draught *(see p79)*.

Top 10 Favorite Local Drinks

1 Singha Beer
Most foreigners pronounce the name of this lager as "Singh-ha," although the proper pronunciation is "Singh."

2 Chang Beer
This potent lager is one of the country's top-selling beers. Equally popular on tourist T-shirts is the Chang elephant logo.

3 Leo Beer
A flavorful lager, Leo Beer is produced by Boon Rawd Breweries.

4 Tiger Beer
Singapore's first locally brewed beer is popular throughout Thailand.

5 Red Bull Cocktails
The energy drink's formula was invented by a Thai businessman, who still owns 49 per cent of the company.

6 "Buckets"
Be wary of this potent Thai specialty, a mix of alcohol, cola, and Red Bull in a bucket, meant to serve a group.

7 Sangsom
Despite its reputation as a Thai whiskey, the liquor is in fact a rum.

8 Phuket Beer
The bottle's logo features a brightly-colored hornbill, perched near Phuket's Phromthep Cape.

9 100 Pipers
This popular western-style whisky is imported from (although not bottled in) Scotland.

10 San Miguel Light
This brew from the Philippines can be found widely throughout Thailand, including Phuket.

Left **Phuket Fantasea stage show** Center **Snake show, Phuket** Right **Bangla Boxing Stadium**

TOP 10 Entertainment Venues

Phuket Fantasea

A spectacular stage show starring not only trapeze artists and traditional dancers, but also dozens of roosters, costumed elephants, and water buffaloes, Phuket Fantasea tells the story of Thailand's exotic heritage. Before the show, you can visit a theme park filled with games and shops, and enjoy elephant rides *(see p76)*.

Simon Cabaret

Phuket's most popular cabaret features outrageous costumes and sets, along with a flamboyant cast of transvestite performers. Since 1991, Simon Cabaret has promised male guests they will arrive relaxed but leave confused, because the performers are "more of a man than you'll ever be, and more of a woman too!" ◈ *Sirirach Road, Patong Beach • Map P2 • 07634 2011 • Open 7:30–9:30pm daily • Adm • www.phuket-simoncabaret.com*

Playhouse

This upscale Patong dinner theater serves delicious three-course Thai and European meals, followed by a colorful cabaret show starring eight chorus dancers. The intimate theater enjoys a reputation for its attentive service and refined environment; the food receives high marks. You can opt for dinner and the show, or just come to watch the show. ◈ *120 Rad Uthit Road, Patong • Map P1 • 07634 1500 • Adm*

Patong Boxing Stadium

Phuket's top venue to watch *muay thai* presents real fights every Monday and Thursday night. Foreigners who train at the local gyms frequently get onto the cards against each other, or local Thai boxers, and these fights are often among the most exciting. Early fights pit younger, lightweight boxers against one another; the bouts gradually build up to the main event *(see p14)*.

A *muay thai* fight, **Patong Boxing Stadium**

Bangla Boxing Stadium

The upper deck seats at Bangla Boxing Stadium look straight down at the action, and are close enough that an uppercut glancing off a boxer's jaw might make you leap out of your seat. These are the best seats in the house. Fight promoters cruise through the streets of Patong in pickup trucks during the afternoon, promoting the fights of the day with loud *muay thai* music *(see p14)*.

A fire dancer on Loh Dalum Beach

Fire Dancing
Popular on Ko Phi Phi's beaches, particularly around Loh Dalum, this rare performance art features flaming staffs and poi spinning in the darkness of the night to pulsating music. To watch these glowing rays of light is mesmerizing, and in photographs, the fire dancers often appear to be playing with halos.

Snake Shows
The audience looks on as a deadly cobra has venom extracted from its razor-sharp fangs into a clear plastic cup. At one of Phuket's unforgettable snake shows, visitors also witness a snake handler kissing a cobra between its eyes, while another handler uses his teeth to pick up a viper. Get your camera ready and don't flinch. You can also have your picture taken with a massive boa constrictor. S *Phuket Shooting Range, 82/2 Patak Road • Map J4 • 07638 1667 • www.phuket-shooting.com*

Phuket Zoo Shows
Three exciting animal shows thrill audiences of all ages. In one performance, macaque monkeys that once worked as coconut pickers ride tricycles and slam-dunk basketballs. In another show,

elephants display their balancing skills, standing on two feet and then sitting like humans. The last show has a brazen zookeeper placing his head inside the gaping jaws of an alligator. S *23/2 Moo 3, Soi Palai, Chaofah Road • Map J4 • 07637 4424 • Open 8:30am–6pm daily • www.phuketzoo.com*

Bangla Road
For people-watching, it's tough to find a setting more outrageous than the night scene on Bangla Road. At once seedy and harmless, this central vein of Patong is filled with beer bars, club promoters, high-heeled girls, and pleasure-seeking travelers from every corner of the globe. S *Map N2*

Go-Go Bars
Patong, in particular Bangla Road, is well known for its many adult venues. Club promoters stroll the street with programs describing what will be on stage that night. Always use your best judgment when entering any bar, and make sure you ask for prices before ordering.

Left **ATVs lined up for rent** Center **Sunbathing, Kata Beach** Right **Rock climbing, Ko Phi Phi**

TOP 10 Outdoor Activities

1 Sunbathing
With so many white-sand beaches and resort pool decks, finding a sunny spot to catch a tan on Phuket does not require much effort. Remember to apply sunscreen; the tropical sun burns, even on cloudy days.

2 Motorbike Rides
Cruise on the hilly coastal roads of western Phuket, passing scenic viewpoints, elephant trekking trails, and tropical foliage. Motorbikes can be rented in many tourist areas. Roadside petrol stands sell fuel in old whiskey bottles. Remember to always wear a helmet.

3 Golf
Phuket is one of Thailand's top golfing destinations, thanks to its picturesque and challenging courses. The Blue Canyon Country Club's *(see p83)* championship course has hosted a number of professional tour events.

4 Elephant Trekking
Sitting atop an elephant as it plods along jungle trails is an unforgettable experience. These animals maintain their balance even on steep downhill terrain. The elephant keeper sits astride the animal's neck, while you ride on a special chair. ◈ *Siam Safari Nature Tours, 45 Chao Far Road, Chalong • 07628 0116 • www.siamsafari.com*

5 Trekking
Thailand's scenic jungle paths lead hikers past waterfalls and lush flora, full of wild orchids and ferns. The Khao Phra Thaeo National Park *(see pp16–7)* has a scenic trail, and at Khao Sok National Park *(see pp26–9)*, you can trek through jungles and bamboo forests.

6 Cycling
Cycling through Phuket's countryside is a great way to explore and to get some exercise on a holiday. Half-day, full-day, and overnight tours through breathtaking scenery also allow cyclists to meet locals. ◈ *Amazing Bike Tours Thailand • 07628 3436 • www.amazingbike toursthailand.asia*

7 Horseback Riding
Horseback rides on Phuket are a great experience. Mornings and late afternoon are the best time to

Golf course on Phuket Island

saddle up, since midday can be very hot. Beginners can hire guides. ✪ *Phuket Riding Club, 95 Viset Road, Rawai • Map H5 • 07628 8213 • www.phuketridingclub.com*

Horseback riding on the beach

Bungee Jumping
Those seeking an adrenaline fix can plunge down a beautiful lagoon in Kathu's bungee jumping site. Jungle Bungy offers standard leaps, tandem dives, and touch water dives. Jumpers are awarded certificates of courage. ✪ *Jungle Bungy Jump, 61/3 Wichitsongkram • 07632 1351 • www.phuketbungy.com*

ATV Touring
All-terrain vehicles are an exciting way to see local villages, farms, and off-the-beaten-path sights. Phuket ATV Tour includes an option to go white-water rafting in Phang Nga, or to experience a ropes course. Wear sports clothes and closed-toe shoes. ✪ *Phuket ATV Tour, 59/26 Moo 5, T. Srisuntorn • 07661 7747 • www.atvphuket.com*

Rock Climbing
With more than 30 climbing routes, Tonsai Tower in Ko Phi Phi also features a number of easy routes which make it ideal for beginners. It also offers courses on how to belay, lead climb, and multi-pitch. ✪ *Spidermonkey Climbing, Ko Phi Phi • 0756 1026 • www.spidermonkeyphiphi.com*

Top 10 Activities for Rainy Days

1 Cooking Classes
Learn to make delicious traditional Thai food at one of the island's many local cooking schools.

2 Thai Massage
This ultra-relaxing form of massage involves stretching and deep, but not painful, pressure.

3 Spa Treatment
With its legendary hospitality, Thailand has earned a reputation as one of Asia's top spa destinations.

4 Museums
Phuket's rich tin mining history can be seen through exhibits at a number of local cultural museums.

5 Temples
Visit one of Phuket's 40 Buddhist temples to observe local monks performing traditional ceremonies.

6 Batik Painting Class
Visit a batik gallery and create your own version of the popular southeast Asian fabric art.

7 Shopping
Rain or shine, the street markets are always open; or visit one of Phuket's many indoor shopping complexes.

8 Phuket Shooting Range
Indoor and outdoor shooting ranges offer target practise for gun lovers of all ages.

9 Cinema
SF Cinema City, located at Jungceylon in Patong, offers five theaters showing the latest releases.

10 Bowling
A modern bowling alley with 16 lanes is located at SF Cinema City.

Left **Speedboats at Chalong Tourist Pier** Center **Jet-skiing in Patong** Right **Kayaks on a beach**

Marine Activities

Swimming
A translucent shade of turquoise, delightfully warm, and fringed by soft sand, Phuket's ocean has for decades made the island one of the world's favorite tropical destinations. Whether you swim at bustling Patong or idyllic Yanui, Phuket's beaches provide postcard-perfect surroundings.

Snorkeling
Almost every beach here has snorkeling opportunities. Rent masks, fins, and snorkels from one of the beachfront rental shops. Alternatively, take boat trips to the popular shallow water reefs surrounding Phuket.

Parasailing
As the speedboat accelerates, your parachute pulls you up into the sky to enjoy staggering over-head views of emerald waters and green hills. If you are scared,

Parasailing off Patong Beach

consider the boy guiding the parachute above you who isn't even wearing a harness.

Kayaking
Explore Phang Nga Bay's extraordinary sea caves in a kayak. Rock tunnels lead into lagoons surrounded by jungles with hornbills, kingfishers, and even monkeys. John Gray's Sea Canoe has been leading eco-friendly canoe trips since 1983. ◈ *John Gray's Sea Canoe, 124 Soi Yawarat • 07625 4505–7 • www.johngray-seacanoe.com*

Jet-Skiing
Glide across the ocean's surface before ramping off a wave and plunging into the water. Many visitors love to jet-ski during their holiday, and most of the major beaches rent them out. However, other than life preservers, little else is offered for your safety.

Deep-Sea Fishing
The Andaman Sea offers anglers an opportunity to cast for all kinds of big-game fish, from prized marlins and sailfish to hard-fighting tuna and giant trevally. Most sportfishing off Phuket operates on a catch-and-release policy. ◈ *Phuket Fishing Charters 48/12 Soi Sunrise, Chalong • 08137 03181 • www.phuketfishingcharters.com*

Surfing
Though not one of the world's primary surfing desti-nations, Phuket's west coast nonetheless offers ample

opportunities to catch a wave. Both Kata and Bangtao beaches host several annual surfing and windsurfing competitions. Other surf spots include Kalim, Naiharn, and Surin beaches.

Sailing
8 Cruise to uninhabited islands with pearly sand beaches, palm trees, and blue waters. Chartered yacht and sailboat trips offer travelers an opportunity to explore secluded beaches and other unspoiled locations in the Andaman Sea. *Phuket Sail Tours: 199/20 Moo 5, Srisoonthorn, Thalang • 087 397 0492 • www.phuketsailtours.com*

A scuba diver near a coral reef

Scuba Diving
9 The Andaman Sea's dive sites are among the best in the world. With crystal clear visibility, rock formations, gorgeous coral reefs, and abundant sea life, the ocean here provides enchanting underwater scenery for divers.

Phuket Wake Park
10 Since 1997, Phuket's only wake park has given wake-boarders and water skiers an ideal setting to hone their skills. Skiers can practice on ramps, kickers, and slide rails. *Phuket Cable Ski, 86/3 Moo 6, Vichitsongkram Road, Kathu • 07620 2527 • Open 9:30am–sundown daily • www. phuketwakepark.com*

Top 10 Big Game Fish in Phuket

1 Sailfish
The ocean's fastest fish migrates through waters near Phuket during the summer months.

2 Yellow Fin Tuna
These beautiful, powerful fish have long been among anglers' favorite prey.

3 Dogtooth Tuna
These massive fish dwell near elevated tropical reef pinnacles in the deep waters around Phuket.

4 Dorado
Sometimes known as mahi-mahi, these surface-dwelling, ray-finned fish are fantastically colorful.

5 Giant Trevally
Though not physically huge, the Giant Trevally puts up one of the toughest fights in the sea.

6 Wahoo
The meat of the Wahoo, a prized big-game fish, is considered a delicacy by many gourmet cooks.

7 Spanish Mackerel
With its razor-sharp teeth, this fish often cuts its way through trolling bait.

8 Barracuda
This toothy, ray-finned fish eats almost everything. It is known for its scary appearance.

9 Black Marlin
One of the most prized captures in the Asia Pacific, the black marlin makes for the perfect trophy.

10 Grouper
The biggest grouper ever caught off Phuket, captured with shark bait, weighed nearly 198 lbs (90 kgs).

Left **Vibrant Phuket Fantasea show** Right **Visitors in the Phuket Aquarium**

🔟 Children's Activities

Phuket Fantasea
A magical, Disney-like production, the colorful Phuket Fantasea show thrills young audiences with its live animal acts, including dozens of costumed elephants. Kids will also enjoy playing carnival games, riding elephants, and witnessing exciting parades, pageants, and street shows at the theme park. The enormous Golden Kinnaree Buffet satisfies even the pickiest of eaters (see p76).

Elephant Rides
Kids can go for an elephant safari, which gives them the chance to take photographs with the animals, followed by the highlight – sitting atop a special padded chair tied to the elephant's back as it plods across Phuket's picturesque jungle trails. Siam Safari is renowned for taking excellent care of its animals.
🐘 Siam Safari Nature Tours: 17/2 Soi Yod Sanae, Chao Far Road, Chalong • 07638 4456 • www.siamsafari.com

Taking an elephant ride in Phuket

Splash Jungle Waterpark
With twisting waterslides, a thrilling wave pool, and the 1,100-ft (335-m) long lazy river, this water-theme park (see p86) in northern Phuket offers an exciting way to spend a sunny day. In the Boomerango water slide – one of the park's signature slides – you plunge down, through a tube, into the Super Bowl, swishing up and down the side walls before hitting the splashdown pool.

Mini-Golf at Dino Park
Located at the Marina Phuket resort complex, this 18-hole miniature golf course navigates around a swamp, lava cave, waterfall, erupting volcano, and a roaring Tyrannosaurus Rex. A fun environment for a competitive round of putting, it also has a theme bar and restaurant.
🦕 Marina Phuket Resort, Karon Beach • Map H4 • 07633 0625 • Open 10am–midnight daily • Adm • www.dinopark.com

Phuket Aquarium
Set on a scenic bay, this aquarium houses more than 150 freshwater and saltwater species, including electric eels, octopuses, sharks, sea turtles, and stingrays. Displays educate visitors about Thailand's rivers, lakes, endangered coral reefs, and mangroves. More than 300,000 people visit the aquarium each year. 🐠 Sakdidet Road, Cape Panwa • Map K5 • 07639 1126 • Open 8:30am–4:30pm daily • Adm • www.phuketaquarium.org

Go Karting

6 Go Karting
With kids' karts reaching speeds up to 25 mph (40 kmph), and specially-designed karts driven by an adult with a child's passenger seat, the Patong Go-Kart Speedway frequently hosts Mini Grand Prix races, including competitions for kids. ◈ *Patong Go-Kart Speedway, 118/5 Vichitsongkram Road, Kathu • Map H2 • 07632 1949 • Open 10am–7pm daily • Adm • www.gokartthailand.com*

Crocodile show at the Phuket Zoo

7 Phuket Zoo
The most popular attractions at this facility *(see p59)* are the live animal shows in which monkeys ride tricycles, elephants stand on two feet, and a zookeeper places his head inside a crocodile's mouth. The zoo also houses an aquarium, a bird park, and an orchid garden. Visitors can take photographs with animals.

8 Paintball
This sport provides an adrenaline rush with little risk of injury. The Phuket Shooting Range offers two fields for competition: the Wood Field is perfect for "capture the flag" games, while the Small Town field lets players simulate urban warfare. Protective headgear and eyewear are provided. Guests can also visit the gun and archery ranges. ◈ *Phuket Shooting Range: 82/2 Patak Road • Map J4 • 07638 1667 • Open 9am–6pm daily • Adm • www.phuket-shooting.com*

9 Phuket Butterfly Garden and Insect World
At this garden, visitors encounter more than 6,000 exotic butterflies that are bred each month. The facility *(see p9)* was established to preserve rare and endangered species. The insect exhibition displays termites, ants, scorpions, and more. Family packages include a welcome drink, plus free butterfly and fish food.

10 Aqua Zone Marine Park
Located near Soi Bangla, these 13 inflated floating play stations are housed in a roped-off section of sea protected from motorized marine traffic. The park offers a climbing mountain, trampoline, waterslide, and seesaw. ◈ *Patong Beach • Map N2 • Open Dec–Apr: 9:30am–6pm daily • Adm*

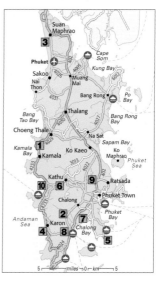

Left **Clothes for sale, Kata Plaza** Center **Night market, Patong** Right **Souvenirs, Thalang Road**

Markets and Shopping Areas

Patong Night Market
At sundown, vendors throughout Phuket set up make-shift tables and tents to peddle everything from handicrafts to DVDs. Patong's Night Market in particular turns the entire town into one big, sprawling night bazaar *(see p15)*.

Kata Plaza
Head here for a selection of watches, sunglasses, and beach-wear, as well as row after row of quality T-shirts. Bargaining is always possible, and sometimes even expected. Kata Plaza is best visited at night; daytime can be insufferably hot here. ◎ *Map H4*

Thalong and Dibuk Roads
These charming streets in old Phuket Town offer many fantastic boutique shops tucked inside historical buildings selling Chinese embroidery, antiques, carved wooden figurines, and regional products from Laos, Cambodia, and Burma. ◎ *Map P5*

Phuket Town Night Market
With lower prices than Patong, Kata, and Karon, the night market in Phuket Town offers the same selection of T-shirts, fishermen's pants, and woodcarvings, as well as second-hand clothes and Thai music albums. ◎ *Map P5*

Plaza Surin
For high-end boutiques, visit Plaza Surin's 12 stores that sell unique items, such as Thai furnishings, original artwork, natural spa products, and cutting-edge audiovisual products. The upscale Silk Restaurant and Bar *(see p55)*, serves delicious Thai cuisine. ◎ *Map A6 • Open 9am–8pm daily*

Chatuchak Weekend Market
Located south of Phuket Town, this massive open-air bazaar *(see p8)* sells soaps, candles, photo frames, sculpture, beachwear, flip-flops, used shoes, puppies, and almost anything else you can imagine. It also has dozens and dozens of food stands selling Thai food.

Turtle Village Shopping Centre
This upscale shopping center in Mai Khao gives northern Phuket shoppers a trendy new place to buy unique Thai souvenirs. Turtle Village offers luxurious Jim Thompson silk, original artwork,

Temporary stalls at the Phuket Town Night Market

jewelry, pearls, seashells and more. ⬦ *Map B2 • Open 9am–10pm daily*

Jungceylon

Anchored by a Robinson department store and a French supermarket, Jungceylon – a massive international shopping destination in Patong – features more than 300 shops selling everything from sports clothes to perfumes and luxury cosmetics. ⬦ *Map P2 • Open May–Oct: 11am–10pm daily; Nov–Apr: 11am–11pm daily • www.jungceylon.com*

Colorful facade of Jungceylon

Canal Village

Surrounded by casuarina trees, the boutiques here are located inside the Laguna Resort complex, but you don't need to be a hotel guest to shop here. Stores include a Silk Factory outlet, Siam Crafts, plus sunglasses and shoe stores. ⬦ *Map B6 • Open 10am–10pm daily*

Phromthep Cape Market

The best souvenir from this popular viewpoint might be the one you take on your camera. You will, however, also find a wide selection of beachwear, handicrafts, seashells, and original artwork in the cape's outdoor markets. The best time to arrive is late afternoon, before the crowds start pouring in (see p20).

Top 10 Exotic Fruits in Phuket

1 Mangosteen

This fruit's *(mang khut)* thick, red skin encloses sweet, slightly tart, and creamy white segments inside.

2 Mango

No Thai holiday is complete without trying sweet mango *(ma muang)* with sticky rice.

3 Lychee

A major Thai export, the lychee's *(lin jee)* thin, hard skin encloses a thick layer of sweet flesh surrounding a small seed.

3 Longan

Covered with a crisp skin, this fruit's *(lam yai)* sweet flesh resembles that of a lychee.

4 Dragon Fruit

This wonderful pink fruit *(geow mangon)* is shaped like a flower and has a light, sweet, and crunchy flesh.

6 Durian

The world's smelliest fruit (durian) isn't permitted inside some hotels. The creamy yellow flesh inside is considered an acquired taste.

7 Banana

Gluay hom (literally, fragrant banana) is used for making delicious desserts and banana cakes.

8 Pomelo

Somewhat like an Asian grapefruit, this citrus fruit *(som oh)* features in the excellent Thai salad *yam som oh*.

9 Rambutan

An interesting-looking fruit, the rambutan *(ngo)* features a hairy red exterior covering sweet, oval-shaped flesh.

10 Rose Apple

This decorative bell-shaped fruit *(chompoo)* has glossy pink skin, with crisp, juicy, and acidic flesh inside.

Left **Seashells on sale** Center **Souvenirs, Jim Thompson shop** Right **Charms, Amulet Market**

🔟 Places to Buy Souvenirs

Night Markets
A variety of inexpensive souvenirs, from mini-elephant figurines to wooden Buddha wall carvings, can be found in Phuket's night markets. Don't forget to bargain, since most items can be bought for half (or less) the seller's initial price *(see p66)*.

Soul of Asia
This magnificent gallery is housed in two old Chinese shop houses and has an impressive selection of rare and antique Asian master paintings, Buddha images, and Asian antiques, including Chinese antique rugs and exquisite Chinese porcelain *(see p87)*.

Jim Thompson
Thailand's leading fine silk brand is named for the American business tycoon who revived, and later epitomized, the Thai silk industry. There are six Jim Thompson shops on Phuket, including one at the airport. You will be sure to find the perfect Thai gift among the neckties, blouses, handbags, and decorative pillows. ® *www.jimthompson.com*

Original Artwork
Artists sell original paintings and reproductions at street-side galleries throughout Phuket. The quality varies, and the costs are always negotiable. The artists often sit at their easels while customers browse the collections.

Bespoke Tailors
Feel like a king as one of Phuket's bespoke tailors, commonly found in Patong, Kata, and Karon beaches, measures you for a custom-fit suit. Just don't wait until the end of your holiday; several fittings are needed to make your suit fit just right.

Buddha statues on display at Chan's Antique House

Chan's Antique House
Phuket's largest collection of art and antiques is housed in this upscale gallery selling Thai home decorations, bronze Buddha statues and vases, teakwood furniture sets, and decorative cabinets. ® *99/42, Moo 5, Chalermprakiat, R 9 Road* • Map J2 • *www.chans-antique.com*

Amulet Market

This bustling marketplace is crowded with Thai and foreign Buddhists sifting through good-luck jewelry. Some amulets were carved by revered monks, or blessed by them. Rare pieces can command prices upwards of B100,000. ⊗ *Map P5*

Necklaces made with locally produced pearls

Phuket Pearls

Choose from the range of white, black, or cream colored pearls, produced on local pearl farms, available at Phuket's markets. You can see how pearls are cultured and extracted at Naka Noi island, off Phuket's north-eastern coast. ⊗ *Phuket Pearl Factory: 58/2 Moo 1, Tambon Kohkaew • Map L1 • 07623 8002 • www.phuketpearl.com*

Traditional Thai Furniture

Furniture made of crushed bamboo, recovered teak wood, rattan, water hyacinth, and more can be found in many shops. Island Furniture can recreate pieces from sketches or photographs. ⊗ *Island Furniture: 90/4 Moo 2, Chao Fah West Road • Map J3 • 07626 3707 • www.islandfurniture-phuket.com*

Seashells

The best place to find rare seashell specimens, or handicrafts made of seashells, is the Phuket Seashell Museum in Rawai. The night market at Phromthep Cape also has a great selection of beautiful shells. ⊗ *Map H5*

Top 10 Bargaining Tips

1 Have fun
Approach your shopping experience lightheartedly – you'll enjoy yourself more.

2 Smile
A friendly smile goes a long way toward ingratiating local salespeople.

3 Don't Lose Your Head
Don't let your negotiations get too serious, and never raise your voice – it's a taboo in Thailand.

4 Be Patient
Don't buy something from the first stall you visit. In Phuket, you'll almost always see it again.

5 Compare Prices
Get price quotes from different vendors selling the same goods; occasionally one vendor's prices are much lower than the others.

6 Buy In Bulk
Sellers often reduce their prices substantially if you buy more than one item.

7 Politely Ask For Discounts
The initial asking price is often about twice as high as the seller's settling price.

8 Walk Away
The classic strategy – say "No, thank you," and walk away. The vendor will often stop you and accept the price you offered.

9 Use Your Head
Avoid too-good-to-be-true prices, especially for expensive items like gemstones or antiques.

10 Currency Exchange
Memorize your exchange rate so you can quickly calculate the cost in your home currency.

Left **Ko Phing Kan, Phang Nga Bay** Right **Resort at Ko Maphrao**

TOP 10 Day Trips

1 Ko Hae
Located just 2 miles (3 km) off Phuket's southeastern shore, Ko Hae, or Coral Island, is a pretty island surrounded by colorful coral reefs. The island has two long sandy beaches – Long Beach and Banana Beach. The most popular activity here is exploring the vast Staghorn coral reefs, located around 328 ft (100 m) offshore. ◈ *Map J6*

2 Ko Phing Kan
Ever since *The Man With The Golden Gun* was filmed here, few people have referred to this island as Ko Phing Kan *(see p95)*. Today widely known as James Bond Island, it is one of Phuket's most popular daytrips. The famous limestone rock called Ko Tapu, or Nail Island, juts out of the sea nearby.

3 Ko Yao Yai and Noi
These picturesque islands in Phang Nga Bay feature charming thatched-roof homes and rubber plantations, interspersed with vast unspoiled foliage. Accommodation is mostly available on Ko Yao Noi,

the smaller of the two islands. Hire a kayak from your hotel to explore the beautiful rock formations facing the island. Alcohol is generally not sold outside hotel premises. ◈ *Map F3*

4 Ko Maphrao
Boasting magnificent deserted beaches and coves, Ko Maphrao (literally, Coconut Island) is five minutes by boat from Phuket's east coast. Popular activities here include swimming and exploring the coastline's mangrove forests by boat. With just one hotel, the island also offers homestays with local families. ◈ *Map L2*

5 Ko Panyee
With most of the island's *(see p95)* land consumed by a towering limestone rock formation, the famous stilt village here has been built above the shallow waters on the island's southern side. The island's main catch today is tourists, who visit Ko Panyee for its seafood restaurants or to buy the delicious spicy *nam prik kung siap* (shrimp paste).

Boat houses along the rubber tree-lined shores of **Ko Yao Yai**

Ko Rang Yai

Home to the Phuket Pearl Farm, this private island cultivates three different types of pearls for export. Ko Rang Yai also offers outdoor activities, including camping, mini-golf, and an air-gun shooting range. Visitors can watch demonstrations on how pearls are cultured, harvested, and turned into jewelry. The guides also explain how to tell the difference between real and fake pearls. ◉ *Map L1*

Gorgeous Ko Racha

Ko Racha

This renowned diving and snorkeling site offers incredibly clear water. Home to fishermen and farmers, Ko Racha Yai has a few bungalows and small restaurants, and a pretty beach. The lack of development makes this a great place for stargazing at night. Ko Racha Noi is less developed and features rockier shorelines. ◉ *Map E4*

Ko Khai Nok

Another great snorkeling destination, this island also has coral reefs hugging the coastline – the prime underwater attraction here. Brilliantly colored parrotfish can often be spotted. The small swimming cove here features white sand flanked by rocky headlands. Small thatched huts sell towels, T-shirts, and fresh coconut water. ◉ *Map F3*

Rocky beach at Ko Bon

Ko Bon

A 15-minute boat ride from Rawai Beach, this small rocky island features a crescent-shaped beach along the west coast. The beach has a quaint restaurant that serves seafood, Thai, and Western dishes. The island's east coast is owned by Evason Resorts for the exclusive use of their guests. ◉ *Map J6*

Ko Kaew

A Buddha statue facing Phuket greets visitors to this small island, which is visible from Phromthep Cape. A replica footprint of the Lord Buddha makes this a holy pilgrimage site for some monks. On the island's far coast is another Buddhist shrine and *chedi*. ◉ *Map H6*

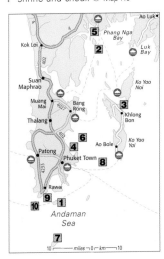

AROUND PHUKET

The South
74–81

The North
82–89

Farther Afield
92–99

PHUKET'S TOP 10

Left **Beautiful Kata Beach** Right **Upscale nightclub, Patong**

The South

O F THE FIVE MILLION TOURISTS WHO VISIT PHUKET ANNUALLY, *the majority flock to Patong, Karon, and Kata on the island's southwest coast. Here, they find an array of world-class restaurants, activities, and hotels all set amid the tropical backdrop of rolling green hills and crystal-blue waters. But most of southern Phuket doesn't pretend to be an escape. Rather, it represents total engagement with its busy beaches, seaside restaurants, open-air bazaars, and throbbing nightclubs. Phuket Town, with its historical architecture, Chinese heritage, and southern Thai cuisine, represents a destination almost wholly distinct from the island's more populated tourist areas*

Colorful umbrellas, Patong Beach

Market stall, Phuket Town

🔟 Sights

1. Phuket Vegetarian Festival
2. Patong Beach
3. Wat Chalong
4. Naiharn Beach
5. Phuket Town
6. Phuket Fantasea
7. Muay Thai
8. Phromthep Cape
9. Big Buddha
10. Kata Beach

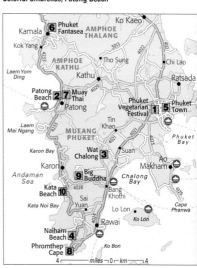

Preceding pages **Boats docked on the shore, Ko Racha**

Phuket Vegetarian Festival

Dating back more than 150 years, the Phuket Vegetarian Festival originated in Kathu after members of a Chinese opera contracted a fatal disease and sought ways to purify themselves and please the gods. For most visitors, the highlight of this entertaining nine-day event are the bizarre acts of piercing and self-mortification practiced by participants, who plunge spears through their cheeks, walk across burning-hot coals, and perform other jaw-dropping displays of self-sacrifice *(see p8)*.

Patong Beach

During the day, sun beds stretch down the entire length of this beach, while watercraft buzz across the bay and parasail riders glide overhead. The island's best dining can be found along the waterfront, with top restaurants commanding impressive views overlooking the bay. The legendary nightlife in Patong needs little introduction. It runs the gamut from pulsating dance clubs to transvestite cabaret shows and open-air beer bars, along with the well-represented adult venues ablaze in neon lights *(see p14)*.

Picture of Luang Pho Chuang, Wat Chalong

Wat Chalong

The island's most famous Buddhist temple, located about 4 miles (6 km) south of Phuket Town, Wat Chalong features a number of brilliantly colored buildings, including a glittering pagoda that supposedly enshrines a bone fragment from the Buddha. During an uprising of migrant tin workers in 1876, the local Siamese fled for protection to this temple, where two monks offered them shelter and helped resolve the dispute peacefully. Today, many Thais visit the statues of Luang Pho Chaem and Luang Pho Chuang in the temple's sermon hall to seek their blessings *(see pp12–13)*.

Naiharn Beach

This picturesque bay on Phuket's far southwestern coast, Naiharn *(see pp20–21)* remains one of the island's better-kept secrets. With just one beachfront resort, the landscape doesn't feel like it has been encroached upon. Tall screw pines populate the area behind the beach, providing a buffer between the nearby Buddhist monastery and Naiharn Lake. The charming Naiharn Town is a short motorbike or car ride from the beach, but is well worth a visit for its cafés, coffee shops, and art studios.

Waterfront restaurants, Patong Beach

Tourism Boom

In the mid-1980s, southern Phuket experienced a wave of development that is widely credited with sparking the island's tourism boom. First, Club Med opened a new resort on Kata Beach in 1985. It proved so popular that THAI Airways soon introduced a daily non-stop flight service from Bangkok to Phuket. The rest is history.

Phuket Town

The cultural and historical sights of Phuket Town offer everything from world-class beaches and natural scenery to a traditional urban home, fascinating 100- year-old Straits Settlements mansions and shop houses, traditional open-air markets and shops, as well as the vividly hued Chinese shrines built during the tin boom of the late 19th and early 20th centuries when thousands of Chinese migrated to Phuket for work. Walking tours are generally the best way to explore the town (see pp8–9).

Phuket Fantasea

This theme park is enough like Disneyland for kids to love it, and enough like Las Vegas for parents to enjoy it too. It is packed with fun activities, entertainment, and shopping. The spectacular Fantasy of a Kingdom is the longest running live show in Asia. Before this dazzling show, you can enjoy one of Asia's largest buffet dinners in the 4,000 seat dining facility at Golden Kinnaree restaurant. ◎ 99 M3 Kamala Beach Kathu • Map G1 • 07638 5000 • Open 5:30pm–11:30pm Fri–Wed • Adm • www.phuket-fantasea.com

A *muay thai* fight, Patong

Muay Thai

Two venues in Patong host regular bouts in which south Thai fighters pummel one another with elbows, shins, knees, and fists. Patong Boxing Stadium and Bangla Boxing Stadium (see p14) witness plenty of vicious knock-outs. The music accompanying the fights sounds like something composed in a madhouse – a haunting windpipe, tribal drums, and tiny finger cymbals encourage the boxers. Many foreign fighters come to train at the *muay thai* gyms on Phuket, and they often test their mettle in the rings here.

Phromthep Cape

On clear nights, a west-facing hilltop on Phuket's southern tip feels like a public gathering in anticipation of what could be a space shuttle launch or a fireworks show, with all eyes on the horizon. However, there is no such spectacle – the crowds are here

Crowds awaiting the sunset, Phromthep Cape

to witness the end of the day, and who'd have thought it could be so spectacular (see p20).

Big Buddha

9 This religious monument on top of Nakkerd Hill has become one of Phuket's iconic landmarks and attracts hundreds of visitors each day. The 148-ft (45-m) tall cross-legged white marble Buddha makes an awesome sight when viewed from sea level, and offers even greater appeal from the hilltop, from where visitors enjoy sweeping views and pleasant breezes. You can also enjoy a sunset dinner at Nakkerd Sea View Restaurant. ☉ Map H4 • Open 8am–7:30pm daily

The magnificent Big Buddha statue

Kata Beach

10 Increasingly upscale, Kata draws positive reviews for the way it harmonizes its tropical beauty with ever-growing crowds and infrastructure. Indeed, the beach here offers many of the same joys as Patong, such as parasailing and jet-skiing, yet it retains a decidedly more relaxed feel. At night, Kata has enough restaurants and nightlife to feel like it's got a pulse, but it isn't overbearing. With a wide selection of shopping, both on the beach and off, it's easy to see why Kata's popularity endures (see pp22–3).

Exploring Phuket's Southwest Coast

Morning

🕐 Start your motorbike journey in **Patong**, the tourist center of the island. Follow the road signs for Highway 4233 towards **Karon**, **Kata**, and **Phromthep Cape**. This coastal road takes you to the island's southern tip. Make your first stop at **Karon Beach**, one of Phuket's largest tourist beaches. Buy a coconut from a beach vendors and enjoy the sweet water inside. Continuing south on the road, you will pass the shop-lined streets of Kata. Stop if something catches your eye. After **Kata Noi**, the road ascends a steep hill that winds its way up to the famous **Karon Viewpoint**, from where you can enjoy breathtaking views and take great photographs, so bring your camera. Continue to **Naiharn**, where a delicious seaside lunch awaits you under the shade of umbrellas and casuarinas behind **Naiharn Beach**.

Afternoon

After a relaxed lunch, follow the road signs to Phromthep Cape. You'll drive around Naiharn Lake, and then up and down a hilly, tree-lined road. At the bottom of the hill is **Yanui Beach**, a charming place to swim, snorkel, and relax under the trees. The road then continues to Phromthep Cape, with its magnificent views over the Andaman Sea. Just be sure to reverse course and reach Patong before it gets too dark. The journey takes about 45 minutes, and you don't want to drive your bike on these roads at night.

Around Phuket – The South

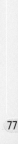

Left **Orchids, Phuket Orchid Farm** Center **Boats moored on Paradise Beach** Right **Tha Rua Shrine**

🔟 Best of the Rest

1 Phuket Orchid Farm

This heavenly nursery and greenhouse displays more than 1,500 different hybrids and species of orchid. ✆ *67/1 Soi Suksan 1, Viset Road, Chalong • Map K2 • 07628 0226 • Open 9am–5:30pm daily • www. phuketorchids.com*

2 Karon Viewpoint

With breathtaking views of the island, this viewpoint is usually populated with vendors selling drinks, snacks, or photo opportunities with exotic birds *(see p22)*.

3 Phuket Zoo

Children love the animal shows starring macaque monkeys, crocodiles, and elephants at the zoo *(see p65)*. You can also have your photograph taken sitting next to a tiger.

4 Phuket Aquarium

Part of the Phuket Marine Biological Center, the Phuket Aquarium introduces visitors to an enchanting underwater world with stingrays, sharks, and sea turtles *(see p64)*.

5 Chinese Shrines

A testament to Phuket's Chinese legacy, the colorful shrines throughout the island play an important role during the Phuket Vegetarian Festival.

6 Ao Sane Beach

This rugged, secluded little beach, not far from Naiharn, offers great opportunities for snorkeling and has a peaceful vibe *(see p21)*.

7 Paradise Beach

Not far from mega-crowded Patong Beach, this delightful little stretch of sand emanates tranquility with its soft sand and palm trees; there is a coral reef not far off shore. ✆ *Map G3*

8 Yanui Beach

This lovely cove *(see p21)* – an ideal setting for kayaking, snorkeling, or reading a book under the shade of palm trees – is located just past the windmill visible from Naiharn Beach.

9 Emerald Beach

With abundant sunshine, this 1,640-ft (500-m) long beach, called Hat Tri Tra in Thai and located south of Patong, offers a quiet place to hide out and work on your tan. ✆ *Map G3*

10 Rawai Beach

A non-swimming beach, Rawai is known for its seafood restaurants along the beach. Speedboats and long-tail boats can be chartered at Rawai to visit the smaller islands nearby. ✆ *Map H6*

Left **The entrance to Molly Malone's, Patong** Right **Bar at the After Beach Bar**

TOP 10 Bars

1 After Beach Bar
A wooden structure with a laid-back vibe, After Beach Bar is located near Karon Viewpoint and specializes in cocktails.
◈ Highway 4233 • Map H5 • 081 894 3750 • Open 9am–11pm daily

2 Molly Malone's
This spirited Irish pub features live music every night.
◈ 94/1 Thaweewong Road, Patong • Map N2 • 07629 2771 • Open 9am–2am daily • www.mollymalonesphuket.com

3 Roots Rock Reggae Bar
With regular barbeque and live music parties, this funky little reggae bar in Patong also features a small shop selling handmade jewelry, leather bags and belts, and more. ◈ Nanai Road, Patong • Map P2 • 087 271 4656 • Open 1pm–2am daily

4 Easyriders
Motorcycle posters and a Confederate flag hang on a wall behind the stage of this biker-themed bar that draws energetic crowds for its live music. ◈ Off Thai Na Road, central Kata • Map H4 • Open 6pm–2am daily

5 Yoonique Stone Music Café
An eclectic spot, this café features live music and regular theme nights. Jam sessions on Tuesdays and live bands on Fridays regularly draw crowds.
◈ 14/61–62 Sai Yuan Road, Rawai Beach • Map H6 • Open 6pm–2am daily

6 Aussie Bar
If you want to catch a live sports game, the Aussie Bar, which broadcasts sporting events from all corners of the globe, is your best bet.
◈ Bangla Road, Patong • Map N2 • Open 9:30am–2am daily

7 Rock City
A lively venue, Rock City hosts top local and international bands playing classic rock, heavy metal, grunge, and more. There is no cover charge before 11pm.
◈ Bangla Road, Patong • Map N2 • Open 8pm–2am daily

8 Timber Rock
The house band here is considered one of the best on Phuket. There is a small dance floor and seating upstairs.
◈ Yaowarat Road, Phuket Town • Map K2 • 07621 1839 • Open 9:30pm–2am daily

9 Kangaroo Bar
This vibrant venue on Bangla Road plays thumping rock music, and offers a free barbeque about once a week. ◈ Bangla Road, Patong • Map N2 • Open early afternoon–2:00am daily • www.kangaroobarphuket.com

10 Banana Disco
Located on the beach road, this is one of Phuket's oldest discos. The high-energy house music played here draws hordes of late-night revelers. ◈ Beach Road, Patong • Map N2 • 07634 0301 • Open 9pm–4am daily

Left **China Inn Café and Restaurant** Center **Kra Jok See** Right **Diners at Thungkha Kafae**

Places to Eat in Phuket Town

1 China Inn Café and Restaurant

The magnificent exterior of this shop house *(see p10)* gives way to a leafy courtyard, where diners enjoy remarkable Thai and Western cuisine, along with delightful Thai desserts. Ⓢ BBB

2 Dibuk Grill and Bar

Serving authentic Thai and French cuisine, and offering a full selection of fine wines, this elegant but relaxing restaurant *(see p10)* is set inside a traditional Straits Settlement house. Ⓢ BBB

3 Anna's Café

This restaurant serves upscale Thai food family-style. The *massaman* (beef curry) and *gaeng som* (sour curry) are two of the most popular dishes here. Ⓢ *Rasada Road • Map P5 • 07621 0535 • Open 6pm–midnight Mon–Sat • BBB*

4 Kopitiam by Wilai

Charming, with an old-fashioned feel and with photographs depicting Phuket in bygone eras, Kopitiam is owned by the same family that runs Wilai (next door). Ⓢ *18 Talang Road, Phuket Town • Map P5 • Open 11am–10pm daily • B*

5 Laemthong Seafood

The oldest Chinese eatery on Phuket is popular for its seafood and Chinese cuisine. Favorites include shark fin soup, oyster omelets, and Peking chicken. Ⓢ *Chana-Charoen Road • Map Q6 • 07622 4349 • Open 11am–10pm daily • BB*

6 Kra Jok See

Set inside a charming old shop house, this Thai restaurant serves foreigner-friendly cuisine, including a delicious steamed seafood curry. Reservations required. Ⓢ *Takua Pa Road, near Rasada Circle • Map N5 • 07621 7903 • Open 6pm–midnight Tue–Sun • BB*

7 Wilai Restaurant

Diners can choose from a selection of pre-cooked curries and stir-fries at this popular spot. *Penang Moo* (coconut milk curry with pork) is highly rated. Ⓢ *Thalang Road • Map P5 • 07622 2875 • Open 7am–2pm daily • B*

8 Ran Jee Nguat

This Chinese-run restaurant serves one of the island's favorite local specialties – *kanom chine naam ya phuket* (Chinese noodles in a puréed fish and curry sauce). Ⓢ *Corner of Yaowarat and Dibuk roads • Map P5 • Open 10am–8pm daily • B*

9 Roti Chao Fa

Delicious curries served with flat bread and numerous exotic teas, help make this small restaurant a popular choice for breakfast. Ⓢ *Chao Fa Road • Map N5 • Open 6am–noon daily • B*

10 Thungkha Kafae

Located on top of Rang Hill, this outdoor café enjoys lovely views and a reputation for the best iced coffee on Phuket. Ⓢ *Top of Rang Hill • Map N4 • 07621 1500 • Open 11am–10pm daily • BB*

Around Phuket – The South

Left **Dish served at Da Maurizio** Center **Attractively located Ratri Italian Bar and Grill**

🔟 Places to Eat in Southern Phuket

1 Da Maurizio Bar Ristorante

An Italian restaurant, Da Maurizio is known for its fish and lobster, imported meats, homemade pastas, and the tasting menu. ⌖ *223/2 Prabaramee Road, Patong Beach • Map P1 • 07634 4079 • BBBB*

2 The Quarterdeck

This restaurant at the Royal Phuket Yacht Club serves Asian and western fare in a casual open-air atmosphere. ⌖ *Naiharn Beach • Map H6 • 07638 0200 • Open 7am–10:30pm daily • BBBB • www.theroyalphuketyachtclub.com*

3 Diavolo Restaurant

Generous á la carte breakfasts and Italian delicacies for lunch and dinner are served here. ⌖ *Paresa Resort, 49 Moo 6, Layi-Nakalay Road, Kamala Beach • Map H4 • 07630 2000 • Open 8am–11pm daily • BBBB • www.paresaresorts.com*

4 Ratri Italian Bar and Grill

Phuket's funkiest upscale restaurant provides memorable Italian bistro-style dishes and amazing views of the Andaman Sea. Live jazz at weekends. ⌖ *Kata Hill • Map H4 • 07633 3538 • BBB*

5 Savoey Seafood

This bustling restaurant offers a massive seafood menu, serving everything from raw oysters to nearly a dozen kinds of fish. ⌖ *136 Thaweewong Road, Patong Beach • Map N2 • 07634 1171 • Open for lunch & dinner daily • BB*

6 Boathouse Wine and Grill

Known for its spectacular wine list, this beachfront restaurant serves popular French and Thai dégustation menus. ⌖ *Kata Beach • Map H5 • 07633 0015 • Open 6:30am–11pm daily • BBBB*

7 Acqua Restaurant

Imaginative dishes feature at this upscale restaurant. It also offers exclusive luxury gourmet trips aboard a yacht. ⌖ *322/5 Prabaramee Road, Kalim Beach • Map N1 • 07661 8127 • Open 4–11pm daily • BBBB*

8 Kan Eang

Located on Phuket's eastern coast, Kan Eang serves classic Chinese-Thai seafood. ⌖ *9/3 Chofa Road, Chalong Bay • Map J4 • 07638 1323 • Open for lunch & dinner daily • BBB*

9 La Gritta

In a quiet bayside setting, this Italian restaurant specializes in gourmet pizzas, handmade pastas, and memorable deserts. ⌖ *Amari Coral Beach Resort, Patong Beach • Map N1 • 07634 0106 • Open 11am–midnight daily • BBB*

10 Lim's Restaurant

On a hill above Kalim Bay, this expat favorite serves modern Thai food in a chic ambience. Good music in the adjacent Nine Lounge Bar. ⌖ *28 Prabaramee Soi 7, Kalim • Map N1 • 07634 4834 • Open 6:30–10:30pm Mon–Sat • BBBB • www.limsphuket.com*

Left **Turtle village, Sirinat National Park** Center **Phuket Boat Lagoon** Right **Flora, Khao Phra Thaeo**

The North

V IRGIN RAIN FOREST, PROTECTED MANGROVES, *wildlife sanctuaries, and unspoiled golden-sand beaches where giant leatherback turtles return each year to lay their eggs – Northern Phuket abounds in opportunities to connect with the area's magnificent natural surroundings. Jungle trekking trails, half-buried golden Buddha statues, and picturesque swimming coves comprise natural wonders, while theme parks, golf courses, and tree-top canopies also attract many visitors. The beaches north of Kamala offer more privacy, tranquillity, and access to nature for those who seek a little more space – and less bustle – during their holiday on Phuket.*

Buddha statues, Wat Prathong

Kayaking in the mangroves, Sirinat National Park

Sights

1 Khao Phra Thaeo National Park

2 Sirinat National Park

3 Wat Prathong

4 Blue Canyon Country Club

5 Phuket Boat Lagoon

6 Laem Singh Beach

7 Gibbon Rehabilitation Centre

8 Elephant and Horseback Rides on Bang Tao Beach

9 Mai Khao Beach

10 Thalang National Museum

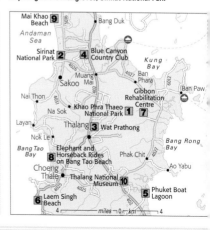

1 Khao Phra Thaeo National Park

Home to numerous protected animal species, as well as rare and exotic plant life, this virgin rain forest features a number of jungle trekking trails, two water-falls, and a gibbon rehabilitation facility. Declared a wildlife sanc-tuary in 1969, Khao Phra Thaeo contains an especially rare palm species called the white-back palm, which was discovered by a German botanist nearly 60 years ago. This unique plant is found only in the park. Animals here include barking deer, gibbons, and flying foxes, as well as snakes and wild pigs *(see pp16–17)*.

2 Sirinat National Park

The pristine shoreline along Phuket's northwestern coast is protected by Thailand's national park service. Every winter, massive sea turtles lay their eggs in the sand here, while virgin mangrove forests can be found at the northern end of the park. An 2,625-ft (800-m) long wooden walkway has been constructed over the mangroves and is a popular scenic walk. The Sirinat National Park protects Mai Khao, Nai Yang, and Nai Thon beaches. The relaxed, natural environs draw a different crowd from the raucous party beaches *(see pp18–19)*.

3 Wat Prathong

The half-buried golden Buddha image here draws worshippers and curious tourists alike. Originally built in the 1750s, Wat Prathong has received high-profile visitors, including King Rama V in 1909. The statue was most likely half-buried as a result of flooding. The reclining gilded Buddha is another popular attraction. The colorful temple complex also features a museum that houses assorted historical items, such as tin mining tools and Javanese daggers, among others. ◎ *Highway 402 • Map C5 • Open 8am–5:30pm daily*

4 Blue Canyon Country Club

Golf aficionados rave about Blue Canyon's rolling fairways, towering trees, and exceptionally well-kept greens. The two pic-turesque championship courses here, the Canyon and the Lakes, are premier golfing destinations. The Canyon Course has hosted the Johnnie Walker Classic three times, playing host to a number of acclaimed golfers. The 17th hole on the Canyon Course is considered one of the 500 best in the world, according to *Golf Magazine*. Non-golfers will enjoy the club's spa and fine dining facilities. ◎ *165, Moo 1 Thepkasattri Road, Thalang • Map C3 • 07632 8088 • www.bluecanyonclub.com*

Clubhouse and golf course, Blue Canyon Country Club

Sea Turtles

During the November to February breeding season, giant sea turtles, including the magnificent leatherback, return to Phuket's northwestern beaches – to the same place they were born – to lay their eggs. Mai Khao and Nai Yang beaches provide perfect nesting sites where sea turtles lay their eggs and bury them in the sand for protection.

Phuket Boat Lagoon

Luxury yachts from around the world are moored in the lagoon here, offering those who don't own vessels to experience the upscale marina lifestyle. Operational since 1994, the Phuket Boat Lagoon features more than 150 units with restaurants, retail outlets, and sport complexes. The Boat Lagoon Resort has 300 guest rooms, exceptional restaurants, tennis courts, swimming pools, and a Thai spa. ◈ 22/1 Moo 2 Thepkasattri Road • Map K1 • 07623 8533-40 • www.phuketboatlagoon.com

Laem Singh Beach

This beautiful, hidden beach, populated by lush palm trees and giant rocks, feels like a secret cove. However, despite being hidden from the road, and the fairly steep path required to reach it, Laem Singh beach remains a popular

Entrance to Canal Village, Bang Tao Beach

spot throughout the year and gets especially busy during high season. The rocky areas in the water provide excellent snorkeling opportunities, while the rustic wooden beach restaurants provide tree-shaded spots to enjoy fresh seafood. ◈ Map G1

Gibbon at the Gibbon Rehabilitation Centre

Gibbon Rehabilitation Centre

Don't expect to hug a baby gibbon and have your photo taken here. Established in 1992, this center seeks to rehabilitate white-handed gibbons in order to reintroduce them into their natural habitat, while at the same time ending the illegal use of these animals as tourist attractions and pets. You can pay a small donation and adopt a gibbon that has been mistreated in captivity. The donation will cover the animal's food and medical care for a year, and you will receive an adoption certificate, a fact file, regular updates, and a T-shirt (see pp16–17).

Elephant and Horseback Rides on Bang Tao Beach

Visitors can ride horses and elephants from the Phuket Laguna Riding Club on the beautiful golden sands of Phuket's second-longest beach. The experience provides marvelous photo opportunities as the animals walk past the calm waters and stunning scenery. Guests can also feed elephants at the camp near the Canal Village Shopping Centre. ◈ Map B6 • Open 9am– 5:30pm daily • Adm

Mai Khao Beach

Part of Sirinat National Park, this 6-mile (11-km) long beach (see p19) has undulating golden sand lined by palm trees and pines. Development in the area has been severely limited, resulting in resorts that truly respect the beauty of the surroundings. Swimming can get rough during summer, but the beach makes for an excellent scenic trek, and beach walkers often find themselves alone with the birds. The area also has seafood restaurants and upscale shopping.

Thalang National Museum

In 1785, two Siamese women helped defend Phuket against an attack by Burmese soldiers. For their bravery, they were honored with this museum, and the nearby Heroines' Monument. A large 9th-century statue of Vishnu, the Hindu god, stands in the museum's main hallway, while other displays feature the island's tin mining history, its Sea Gypsy communities, and more.
◈ Thalang • Map D6 • 07631 1025
• Open 8:30am–4pm daily • Adm
• www.nationalmuseums.finearts.go.th

Facade of the Thalang National Museum

A Day in Northern Phuket

Morning

Hire a private car for this itinerary if you don't have a rented one, since the journey covers quite a bit of ground. Also carry sturdy shoes, swimwear, and a towel. Start the day auspiciously by making merit at **Wat Phrathong**, where local Buddhists revere the half-buried golden Buddha image. The temple is located quite far inland, so it isn't as crowded as Wat Chalong. Continue eastward to the nearby **Khao Phra Thaeo National Park**, one of the last remaining habitats for exotic animals on Phuket. Here, park your car near **Bang Pae Waterfall** and eat at one of the restaurants near the car park. Better still, buy a takeaway meal and enjoy a picnic in the shade near the waterfall.

Afternoon

A short walk from Bang Pae is the **Gibbon Rehabilitation Centre**, where gibbons who were ill-treated in captivity are reintroduced into a wild habitat. Adopt a baby gibbon for a small amount of money, and ensure that the animal continues to receive vital care. If you're feeling energetic, hike the 5-mile (8-km) long jungle path to **Ton Sai Waterfall**. Otherwise, drive to Bang Pae on the eastern shore to go elephant trekking through the jungles of the national park. When hungry, visit the floating restaurant in the coastal mangrove swamps. Return to your hotel by the early evening.

Left **Laguna Phuket Golf Club** Right **Picnicking at the Nai Yang beach**

TOP 10 Best of the Rest

1 Bang Pae and Ton Sai Waterfalls

The two waterfalls in Khao Phra Thaeo National Park, linked by a hiking trail, are picturesque destinations surrounded by beautiful jungle scenery *(see p16)*.

2 Laguna Phuket Golf Club

Voted one of the best resorts in Asia, this golf club features scenic lagoons and immaculate greens. ✆ *34 Moo 4, Srisoonthorn Road, Cherngtalay • Map B6 • 07632 4350 • www.lagunaphuketgolf.com*

3 Windsurfing in Bang Tao

Bang Tao enjoys the reputation of being one of Phuket's best places to windsurf. Boards and sails can be rented from local resorts and shops. ✆ *Map B5*

4 Wat Mai Khao

A serene and unadorned temple located in a quiet forested area near Mai Khao village, Wat Mai Khao also has a bird sanctuary and a lake within its compound.

5 Heroines' Monument

Located at the Tha Rua roundabout, this monument is a tribute to the sisters who helped defend Phuket from invaders in the 18th century. ✆ *Thepkasattri Road • Map C6*

6 Cable Jungle Adventure Phuket

With 15 stations and a 3,937-ft (1,200-m) long cable run, this treetop canopy adventure gets your adrenaline pumping. ✆ *232/17*

Bansuanneramit, Moo 8, Srisoonthorn Road • 07652 7054 • Open 9am–6pm daily • www.phuketcanopy.com

7 Nai Thon Beach

A sleepy little hideaway, this beach is generally free of large tourist crowds. The reefs here are popular with divers. ✆ *Map A4*

8 Splash Jungle Waterpark

With thrilling rides, this theme park is an ideal place to splash around. ✆ *65 Moo 4, Mai Khao Soi 4, Mai Khao Beach • Map B2 • 07637 2111 • Open 10am–6pm daily • www.splashjunglewaterpark.com*

9 Nai Yang Beach

A popular picnic destination for locals, this tree-lined beach has restaurants that serve a selection of delicious seafood. ✆ *Map B4*

10 Surin Beach

This beach houses some of Phuket's top-end resorts such as The Chedi. The area's wealth is reflected in the neighboring homes and restaurants. ✆ *Map A6*

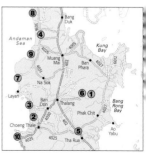

Left **Merchandise at Ginger Boutique** Right **The über-chic Banyan Tree Gallery**

🔟 Places to Shop

1 Soul of Asia
Serious art collectors will be delighted by this massive collection. ✆ *5/50 Moo 3, Cherngtalay • Map A6 • 07627 1629 • www.soulofasia.com*

2 Baru
Baru's flagship store in Phuket offers the best selection of luxury beachwear for women – from bikinis to beach bags and other accessories. ✆ *186/12 Thaveewong Road, Patong Beach • Map N2 • 07634 6425 • www.barufashion.com*

3 Red Coral
This boutique sells necklaces, photo frames, postcards, beach sandals, bags, and more. The unique seashell and pearl products make great gifts. ✆ *Turtle Village, Mai Khao Beach • Map B2 • 07631 4811*

4 Lemongrass House
With some 90 aromas to choose from, the spa products sold here are among the best in Asia. Customers can even blend their own products. ✆ *Srisoonthorn Road, Bang Tao • Map B5 • 07627 1233 • www.lemongrasshouse.com*

5 Banyan Tree Gallery
Showcasing indigenous handicrafts by artisans from around the world, this gallery seeks to conserve traditional crafts and skills. Home furnishings, apparel, spa candles, jewelry, and more can be purchased here. ✆ *Laguna Phuket Resort complex • Map B6 • 07636 2300 • www.banyantreegallery.com*

6 Heritage Collection
Antique wood and bronze Buddha images from southeast Asia along with Chinese sculptures, imperial clothing, and furniture are part of the Heritage Collection. ✆ *106/19–20 Bang Tao Beach Road, Cherngtalay • Map B5 • 07632 5818*

7 Ginger Boutique
A sophisticated boutique, Ginger offers high-end designer jewelry and chic accessories, such as scarves, beaded bags, shoes, and clothing. ✆ *Surin Plaza, 5/50 Moo 3, Cherngtalay • Map A6 • 07627 1616*

8 Fine 9 Design
Enormous shells, vases, ceramic bowls, Thai-style teak wood rattan furniture, and original artwork are sold at this upscale home store at Plaza Surin. ✆ *Surin Plaza, 5/50 Moo 3, Cherngtalay • Map A6 • 07627 1620*

9 Candere Gallery
Original handicrafts and jewelry from around Thailand, and a wide range of high-end home products, can be found in this gallery. ✆ *Second Floor, Plaza Surin, 5/50 Moo 3, Cherngtalay • Map A6 • 07627 1776*

10 The Palace of Art
This showroom displays some of the best examples of genuine Thai, Myanmar, and Cambodian fine art. ✆ *103/3 Moo 4, Banbangjoe • Map A6 • 07627 3533*

Left **Horseback Riding** Center **Kite surfing, Nai Yang Beach** Right **Elephant trekking, Naiharn**

TOP 10 Outdoor Activities

Trekking
Northern Phuket's most scenic trek navigates through 4 miles (6 km) of jungle trails in the Khao Phra Thaeo National Park. Guides can be hired at the visitor center near Bang Pae Waterfall.

Canoeing
Go canoeing in the fantastic mangrove forests and sea caves along Phuket's northeastern and northwestern coasts.

Golfing
Some of Phuket's best golf courses can be found on the island's northern half. Mission Hills, Blue Canyon, and Laguna Phuket each offer picturesque, challenging, and well-maintained courses. ✎ *Map B6*

Snorkeling
There are many opportunities to witness beautiful underwater coral formations and colorful schools of fish in and around Phuket. In winter, the clear waters off Surin, Nai Yang, and Nai Thon make for great dives.

Kite Surfing
With year-round winds, Phuket's west coast is ideal for kite-surfing enthusiasts. Nai Yang Beach, which is free of speed-boats and jet-skis, has a popular school that offers classes for beginners. ✎ *Kitesurfing Phuket, Nai Yang Beach • Map B4 • 081 591 4594 • www.kiteboardingasia.com*

Horseback Riding
The Laguna Riding Club and Phuket Riding Club offer horseback rides along the seashore. The activity is especially popular during the low season when swimming can be dangerous.

Elephant Trekking
Enjoy the unique experience sitting atop a massive pachyderm as it plods down the tropical beach with ocean waves crashing at the animal's toes. ✎ *Laguna Excursions Limited, 390/1 Moo 1, Srisoonthorn Road, Cherngtalay • 07636 2330 • www.lagunaphuket.com*

Bicycling
Experience northern Phuket's back roads and trails on a bicycle tour. A popular trip involves cruising through villages and plantations in the island's northeast. ✎ *Amazing Bike Tours Thailand • 07628 3436 • www.amazingbiketoursthailand.asia*

Camping
Visitors can pitch a tent on parts of Nai Yang and Mai Khao beaches in the Sirinat National Park. The park's visitor center, at the southern end of Mai Khao, rents out tents. ✎ *Map B3*

Swimming
Excellent swimming beaches stretch from Kamala to Mai Khao, on Phuket's northwestern coast. Be cautious during low season, however, as undertows and currents can be strong. Look out for red flags.

Price Categories

For a three-course meal for two with half a bottle of wine (or equivalent meal), taxes and extra charges.

B	under B150
BB	B150–500
BBB	B500–1000
BBBB	over B1000

Left **The kitchen in Cucina** Center **Beachfront restaurant at Sala Phuket**

🔟 Places to Eat

1 Sala Phuket
This resort's beachfront restaurant features candlelit tables and offers fresh seafood, savoury traditional Thai delicacies, and a range of international fare. 🌐 *333 Moo 3, Mai Khao Beach • Map B2 • 07633 3888 • www.salaphuket.com • BBBB*

2 Cucina
Located inside the gorgeous JW Marriott on Mai Khao Beach, this award-winning Italian restaurant serves authentic rustic fare in an old world family trattoria ambience. 🌐 *JW Marriott, 231 Moo 3, Mai Khao Beach • Map B2 • 07633 8000 • www.marriott.com • BBBB*

3 Jakajan Seafood Restaurant
One of the many thatch-roofed restaurants on the beachfront, Jakajan serves fresh seafood in a casual, Thai-style environment. 🌐 *Mai Khao Beach • Map B2 • BB*

4 Catch Beach Club
Specialties in this trendy seaside eatery include the seared tuna with wok-fried vegetables and caper sesame dressing. 🌐 *Surin Beach Road • Map A6 • 07631 6567 • www.catchbeach.com • BBB*

5 Pla Seafood
Illuminated at night by candles and flaming torches, this outdoor spot offers a charming ambience to enjoy fresh seafood and Thai and Austrian cuisine. 🌐 *Surin Beach • Map A6 • 08108 5706 • www.plaseafood.com • BBB*

6 Kin Dee Restaurant
Try the crabmeat stir fried with curry powder at this seafood restaurant. 🌐 *71/6 Moo 5, Mai Khao Beach • Map B2 • 082 814 8482 • www.kindeerestaurant.com • BBB*

7 Casuarina Beach Restaurant & Pub
This fine dining restaurant at Dusit Thani Laguna Phuket Resort is known for its weekly Moon Light Magic BBQ buffet. 🌐 *Dusit Thani Laguna Phuket Resort • Map B6 • 07636 2999 • www.dusit.com • BBBB*

8 Tatonka Restaurant
Influenced by Mediterranean, Asian, and Latino cuisines, the fusion fare here receives high praise from Tatonka's patrons. Specialties include the Sashimi spring rolls and Peking duck pizza. 🌐 *382/19 Moo 1, Cherngtalay • Map B6 • 07632 4349 • BBB*

9 360° Restaurant
Located on a hilltop at The Pavilions Phuket, this romantic eatery is known for its tuna tartar, smoked pork back ribs, and dark chocolate fondue. 🌐 *The Pavilions, 31/1 Moo 6, Cherngtalay • Map B6 • 07631 7600 • www.thepavilionsresorts.com • BBBB*

10 Toto Italian Restaurant
Traditional Italian dishes – homemade pastas, fresh seafood, meats and wood-fired pizzas – make this a popular restaurant. 🌐 *Near the Laguna Phuket Resort entrance • Map B6 • 07627 1430 • BBB*

Left **Visitors setting off for a cruise around the Similan Islands** Right **Shoal of fish, Ko Phi Phi**

Farther Afield

TRY TO IMAGINE THE PERFECT TROPICAL LANDSCAPE, *and you will probably conjure up almost exactly the scenery that surrounds Phuket – unspoiled white-sand beaches, enchanting underwater worlds, ancient rain forests, and dramatic limestone cliffs. There are also hundreds of exotic birds, rare plants and flowers, animals in their natural habitats, colorful coral reefs, and awe-inspiring vistas. Easily accessible from Phuket as daytrips, these locations often represent the road less traveled. Southern Thailand's natural wonders draw millions of visitors each year, but at their farthest reaches – trekking on jungle trails, immersed in the azure sea, kayaking in cave grottoes, or boating through sparsely populated bays – you'll often find yourself alone.*

Trekking in Khao Sok

🔟 Sights

1. Maya Bay
2. Similan Islands
3. Phang Nga Bay
4. Khao Sok National Park
5. King Cruiser Wreck Dive
6. Khao Lak
7. Ko Phi Phi Don
8. Sunrise at Phi Phi Viewpoint
9. Ko Panyee
10. Ko Phing Kan

Preceding pages **Maya Bay, Ko Phi Phi Ley**

1 Maya Bay
Framed on three sides by steep limestone cliffs, and caressed by calm crystal blue waters, this breathtakingly picturesque beach (see p31) on Ko Phi Phi Leh is best known for its appearance in the Hollywood movie, *The Beach*. Though still largely undeveloped, Maya Bay today features camp sites, toilet facilities, and a snack bar for overnight visitors.

Breathtaking Maya Bay

2 Similan Islands
One of the world's premier scuba diving destinations, the Similan Islands (see pp24–5) offer underwater landscapes renowned for their staggering colors and marine life. Even the names of popular dive sites – East of Eden, Richelieu Rock, and Anita's Reef – conjure up images of exotic seascapes. Located in the Andaman Sea, about 31 miles (50 km) from Khao Lak, the Similans are best visited as part of an overnight or multi-day tour. Non-divers can enjoy snorkeling, boat tours, and visits to uninhabited islands.

3 Phang Nga Bay
Dramatic limestone cliffs jut up from this bay (see pp30–31), providing extraordinary scenery for boat cruises, kayak journeys, and island tours. To experience the bay fully, spend an entire day here, venturing beyond the popular tourist sites such as Ko Phing Kan and Ko Panyee. Kayak tours explore cave tunnels that open into fantastic *hongs* (lagoons). Traditional Chinese junk boats, long tail boats, and speedboats can be hired along Phuket's east coast piers, as well as from Chalong and Rawai Beach.

4 Khao Sok National Park
Home to exotic wildlife, including the Malaysian tapir, wild boars, and pig-tailed macaque monkeys, this national park is one of Thailand's most pristine virgin rain forests. The majestic scenery features deep valleys, towering limestone cliffs, lakes, and jungle paths. Adventures into the park often include elephant treks, canoeing, and jeep safaris. The park's picturesque Cheow Laan Lake, framed by verdant cliffs, is home to floating bamboo raft houses, and the area is a favorite with photographers and bird-watchers (see pp26–9).

Turquoise waters around Ko Similan

Around Phuket – Farther Afield

Around Phuket – Farther Afield

Eco Controversy

While *The Beach* was being filmed on Ko Phi Phi in 1999, environmentalists claimed that filmmakers damaged Maya Bay by clearing coconut trees and grass, and altering sand dunes in order to make the beach appear more attractive. The tsunami in 2004, however, essentially washed away all signs of human tampering.

Upscale resort, Khao Lak

King Cruiser Wreck Dive

On May 4, 1997, a ferry making a routine trip from Phuket to Ko Phi Phi collided with a reef pinnacle and sank. The crew and passengers were all rescued. Today the sunken cruiser remains a popular and relatively uncomplicated dive site, reachable with standard scuba gear. The ship features large openings that offer easy access to the boat's interior. ◈ *Map F3*

Khao Lak

Pristine jungles hug the coastline, while the clear waters and white sand beaches of Khao Lak offer a natural paradise for those seeking tranquillity. A number of fascinating diving and snorkeling sites, hidden beaches, and upscale resorts populate Khao Lak. The Khao Sok Lam Ru National Park features beautiful sea cliffs, estuaries, and mangroves. Treks and long tail boat trips can be arranged at the park's visitor center. The 2004 tsunami devastated Khao Lak, but the area has made a strong recovery, and today tourism is flourishing again. ◈ *Map E2*

Ko Phi Phi Don

Once populated by fishermen and later home to vast coconut plantations, this beautiful island southeast of Phuket is now a thriving tourist destination. With colorful bays framed by cliffs and turquoise waters, Ko Phi Phi Don possesses physical beauty but also has a thriving nightlife and many convenience stores. Although the 2004 tsunami destroyed much of Ko Phi Phi Don, it has been almost entirely rebuilt *(see p30)*.

Sunrise at Phi Phi Viewpoint

Enjoy breathtaking views of the sunrise from Ko Phi Phi Don's highest point *(see p31)*, some

Breathtaking view from Phi Phi Viewpoint

610 ft (186 m) above sea level. The island's dumbbell shape can be seen beyond the treetops, as well as the dramatic rock formations on the far side of the island. The journey to the summit doesn't take much time or effort – just 20 minutes or so from Loh Dalum Bay.

Ko Panyee

Most of this small island consists of a massive limestone outcrops that rises vertically out of Phang Nga Bay. The main attraction here is the stilt village constructed in the shallow waters along the island's south side. The island's economy today relies increasingly on daytrippers from nearby Phuket. Fresh seafood restaurants line the shore, and a mosque towers over the village. Visitors often visit Ko Panyee and Ko Phing Kan as part of a packaged tour. ◈ Map F2

Famous Ko Phing Kan

Ko Phing Kan

With Roger Moore as 007, *The Man With The Golden Gun* (1974) placed Phang Nga Bay squarely into the imaginations of movie lovers around the world. Today, mention that you want to visit Ko Phing Kan, and its likely that you'll be met with a confused stare. The island – islands, if you count the vertical limestone formation offshore – is now popularly known as James Bond Island. ◈ Map F3

Daytrip to Ko Phi Phi

Morning

Set your alarm clock for early in the morning, and catch the boat that leaves **Rassada Pier** on Phuket's east coast at 8:30am. Preferably choose a tour company that arranges pickups from your hotel. Onboard the passenger ferry to **Ko Phi Phi**, you can breakfast on coffee, sandwiches, and fresh fruit on the open-air roof deck or in an air-conditioned cabin. After dropping off some travelers at **Ko Phi Phi Don**, the boat continues to the nearby **Ko Phi Phi Leh** and the world-famous **Maya Bay**. Renowned for its gorgeous beaches, emerald waters, and towering cliffs, Maya Bay is very popular with visitors. You can go snorkeling here before visiting other beautiful bays. Visit **Viking Cave**, where swifts build "saliva nests," used for making the delicacy known as bird's nest soup. For lunch, the boat returns to Phi Phi Don, where a Thai and international cuisine buffet awaits you.

Afternoon

After lunch, relax on the famous twin bays of **Ton Sai** and **Loh Dalum**. These beaches have sun beds with umbrellas, while the comfortably warm blue waters remain shallow even more than 328 ft (100 m) from the shore. You can also visit **Monkey Beach**, home to numerous of these curious creatures. It also offers good snorkeling and opportunities to see colorful fish and coral. Take the ferry when it returns to Phuket around 4:45pm, so you'll be back at your hotel in time for dinner.

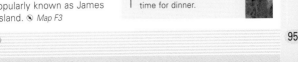

Left **Fire show, Ko Phi Phi** Center **Loh Dalum Beach** Right **Boating, Surin Islands National Park**

ⓂⓄ Best of the Rest

1 Fire Shows, Ko Phi Phi
Flaming staffs and twirling fiery orbs create a tribal feel during the nightly fire shows on the beach on Ko Phi Phi. Ⓢ *Map F3*

2 Ko Yao Noi
Popular for its eco-friendly homestay programs, Ko Yao Noi remains an idyllic and rustic destination in Phang Nga Bay. Visitors appreciate its quiet beaches, slow-paced lifestyle, picturesque hiking trails, and kayaking opportunities. Ⓢ *Map F3*

3 Ko Hae (Coral Island)
Named for the impressive coral reef surrounding the island, this popular day-trip destination located off Phuket's east coast has two beaches. Ⓢ *Map F3*

4 Surin Islands National Marine Park
Most easily accessed from Khao Lak, this chain of islands spans nearly 58 sq miles (150 sq km) of under water area. Pristine under water reefs make this a popular destination for divers. Ⓢ *Map E2*

5 Viking Cave
This cave, at Ko Phi Phi Leh, has ancient carvings resembling Viking-style vessels. These petroglyphs confirm the legends of Viking boats visiting the Andaman coast below. Ⓢ *Map F4*

6 Camping on the Beach at Ko Similan
The tent campgrounds on Ko Similan allow visitors to spend a night on the beach, listening to the waves gently tumbling on shore. Ⓢ *Map D2*

7 Monkey Beach
While some come to Ko Phi Phi to take photographs of the pesky monkeys on the beach, others come for the snorkeling opportunities at the fabulous reef located just off shore. Ⓢ *Map L5*

8 Loh Dalum Beach
This splendid tropical beach on Ko Phi Phi features limestone cliffs almost encircling a white-sand beach. Ⓢ *Map M6*

9 Nightlife on Ko Phi Phi
Many visit Ko Phi Phi for its natural beauty. Another major draw is the island's legendary nightlife, which includes everything from cocktail buckets and beach bars to fire dancing. Ⓢ *Map F3*

10 Stargazing on Ko Similan
On cloudless nights, innumerable stars, constellations, and even planets punctuate the dark sky above the Andaman Sea, presenting a rare opportunity to clearly witness the incredible cosmos. Ⓢ *Map D2*

Price Categories

For a three-course
meal for two with half
a bottle of wine (or
equivalent meal), taxes
and extra charges.

B	under B150
BB	B150–500
BBB	B500–1000
BBBB	over B1000

Left **Cocktail at Carpe Dium** Center **Entrance to Matt's Joint**

TOP 10 Places to Eat on Ko Phi Phi

1 Pee Pee Bakery
This popular breakfast spot serves fresh doughnuts, pastries, and coffee, as well as decent Thai and Western food. ⊗ *Tonsai Village • Map F3 • Open 8am–2am daily • B*

2 Le Grand Bleu
Serving excellent French cuisine and with a decent wine list, this upscale restaurant has an elegant ambience that receives high praise. ⊗ *Tonsai • Map F3 • 081 979 9739 • Open 6:30–11pm daily • BBB*

3 Chao Koh Restaurant
With seating for more than 300 people, this bustling beachfront restaurant serves fresh seafood, including swordfish, barracuda, and grouper. ⊗ *Tonsai • Map F3 • 07560 1083 • Open 7am–10:30pm daily • BB*

4 Carpe Diem
Located at Phi Phi Village Resort, this beachside eatery serves Thai and Western favorites. At night, Carpe Diem goes into party mode with cocktail buckets and fire shows. ⊗ *Eastern Tonsai • Map F3 • Open 8–2am daily • BBB*

5 Ciao Bella
An Italian restaurant on the beach, Ciao Bella serves excellent pizzas and decent homemade pastas. The charming surroundings have a relaxed vibe and diners appreciate the fresh ocean breezes. ⊗ *Loh Dalum • Map M6 • 081 894 1246 • Open 10:30am–10:30pm daily • BB*

6 Cosmic
Delicious pizzas, homemade pastas, and Thai food attract the hungry hordes to this popular restaurant. The wood-fired pizzas here are irresistible. ⊗ *Tonsai • Map F3 • BB*

7 Pum Restaurant & Cooking School
Not only can you eat delicious Thai food here, but you can also learn how to prepare it in a cooking school run by the owner. ⊗ *Tonsai • Map F3 • 081 521 8904 • Open 11am–10pm daily • www. pumthaifoodchain.com • BB*

8 Papaya
Run by a former *muay thai* boxer, the wildly popular Papaya serves mouth-watering Thai curries, *somtam* (spicy papaya salad), and *pad thai* (stir-fried rice noodles). ⊗ *Tonsai • Map F3 • Open 11am–2pm daily • B*

9 Song's Pad Thai
Customers' compliments are scribbled onto note pads and affixed to the walls of this popular spot for *pad thai*. ⊗ *Tonsai • Map F3 • Open noon–11pm daily • B*

10 Matt's Joint
Real Australian beef burgers and steaks, as well as fresh seafood, draw crowds to this bustling restaurant in central Tonsai. Matt's Joint also has a decent selection of Australian wines. ⊗ *Tonsai • Map F3 • Open noon–11pm daily • BB*

Left *Muay thai* fight, Reggae Bar Center Apache Beach Bar Right Rolling Stoned Bar

TOP10 Nightlife on Ko Phi Phi

The Stones Bar
Relax on floor cushions in this chilled out bar that plays house music. You can also get a bamboo tattoo here. ⊗ *Loh Dalum • Map L6 • Open noon–2am daily*

Carlito's Bar
This is one of the island's biggest party spots. Dance the night away, or join one of the bar's infamous Full Moon or Black Moon parties. Nightly fire shows start around 10pm. ⊗ *Tonsai • Map F3 • Open 8–2am daily*

Bora Bora
Formerly known as Hippies, this beach spot, located in eastern Tonsai, has continued the tradition of spectacular fire shows and after-hours parties. ⊗ *Tonsai • Map F3 • Open 8pm–2am daily*

Reggae Bar
Nightly *muay thai* fights provide the main entertainment at this bustling bar in central Tonsai. The boxing ring here witnesses its fair share of fights and even the occasional barfight. ⊗ *Tonsai • Map F3 • Open 5pm–2am daily*

Banana Bar
The island's only rooftop bar pumps out rock and electronic tunes, while *sheesha* can be smoked in funky huts. You can indulge in some skywatching with the bar's telescope. Arrive early for acoustic music. ⊗ *Tonsai • Map F3 • Open 4pm–2am daily*

Rolling Stoned Bar
Live rock music helped the Rolling Stoned Bar to become an enduringly popular nightspot. Pool tables, dim lights, and floor cushions combine to create a funky, upbeat environment for listening to music. ⊗ *Tonsai • Map F3 • Open 5pm–2am daily*

Ibiza Bar
Another popular party spot, this open-air bar features great dance music and outlandish fire jugglers. Visitors can even try their hands at jumping over a flaming rope. ⊗ *Loh Dalum • Map L6 • Open noon–2am daily*

Apache Beach Bar
Thumping music draws passersby onto Apache's wild dance floor. Body painting, bikini parties, and other events crank up the temperature here. ⊗ *Tonsai • Map F3 • Open 5pm–2am daily*

Beach Bar
Candlelit tables and lanterns makes this bar a perfect spot for romantic couples at sundown. The music picks up as the night progresses. ⊗ *Loh Dalum • Map L6 • Open 9–2am daily*

Velvet Dojo
A hip bar, Velvet Dojo plays a good selection of funky music, while you relax on comfortable sofas and enjoy refreshing cocktails. The bar has a free Wi-Fi facility. ⊗ *Tonsai • Map F3 • Open 2pm–2am daily*

Left **Entrance to P. P. Marijuana Shop** Center **D's Books** Right **T-shirts on sale at a local store**

TOP 10 Shopping on Ko Phi Phi

D's Books
With two outlets in central Tonsai, this is the best place to buy, sell, or trade your books. The outlet next to Reggae Bar doubles as a coffee shop.
🔊 *Tonsai • Map F3*

Same Same
You can rent acoustic guitars from Same Same. Choose from about 15 guitars, and enthrall fellow travelers with your ability to strum and sing a tune.
🔊 *Tonsai • Map F3*

P. P. Marijuana Shop
This well-presented shop (with a misleading name) sells a wide range of interesting hand-made jewelry and souvenirs, including silver bracelets, neck-laces, and earrings. The quality of goods sold here is better than in the markets. 🔊 *Near the pier • Map F3*

Rasita
A boutique for women, Rasita specializes in chic dresses, tops, handbags, and shoes – every-thing a girl needs to show up in style. The shop's interiors even look like a girl's bedroom.
🔊 *Tonsai Village • Map F3*

Markets
The latest films and music can be found on CD and DVD, and computer software and games are also available. Non-pirated goods include clothes and decora-tive items. 🔊 *Tonsai • Map F3*

7-Eleven
Chain convenience stores can be found nearly everywhere on Phuket. If you've forgotten some essentials at home, you can buy whatever you need at one of these stores. 🔊 *Tonsai • Map F3*

Kun Va
Attractive beachwear, including stylish sarongs and other accessories can be found at Kun Va. The quality of products here is better than those avail-able on the beaches. 🔊 *Tonsai • Map F3*

T-shirts
Favourite T-shirts on Ko Phi Phi include local beer shirts (Singha and Chang), as well as the ever-popular, "Same, Same, But Different." 🔊 *Tonsai • Map F3*

Kunstone
This small boutique sells high-quality silver jewelry, such as bracelets, earrings, and other accessories. The selection here makes for attractive gifts.
🔊 *Tonsai • Map F3*

MJ Bamboo Tattoo
Memorialize your visit to Phuket with a traditional bamboo tattoo. Located at two sites in Tonsai, MJ Bamboo Tattoo has artists who can copy a design, create a new one, or allow you to choose from standard designs, including those that offer spiritual protection. 🔊 *Tonsai • Map F3 • 081 797 4450*

STREETSMART

Planning Your Trip
102

Getting There
and Around
103

Security and Health
104

Banking and
Communications
105

Sources of Information
106

Things to Avoid
107

Budget Tips
108

Accommodation and
Dining Tips
109

Specialist Holidays
110

Etiquette Tips
111

Places to Stay
112–117

PHUKET'S TOP 10

Left **Summertime flowers** Center **Visitors at a temple, Phuket** Right **Tourism Authority of Thailand**

🔟 Planning Your Trip

When to Go
Phuket's peak season lasts from November until May. Temperatures rise in April and May before the rainy season, which lasts from June to October. Even during September and October, when rainfall is at its heaviest, Phuket receives plenty of sunshine and island activities continue unabated.

What to Take
You will be able to buy just about anything you need on Phuket, so if you forget something, you can simply go shopping when you arrive. However, it is best to bring prescription medicines from home. If you plan to visit Buddhist temples, wear long pants and shirts that cover your shoulders.

Online Planning
The Tourism Authority of Thailand website provides a wealth of information to help you plan your trip, including interactive maps, suggested itineraries, and special holiday travel deals. Candid reviews of hotels and tour companies can be found on many web message boards, while other sites provide detailed descriptions of beaches, activities, and other attractions. ✆ www.tourismthailand.org

Vaccinations
Immunization against polio, tetanus, hepatitis A and B, and typhoid is recommended. Travelers to remote, rural areas should get vaccinations for Japanese encephalitis, hepatitis B, diphtheria, rabies, and tuberculosis. Rare, local cases of malaria have been reported on Phuket and Phang Nga, but none in the major tourist areas.

Passports & Visas
Many passport holders are granted tourist visa exemptions, valid for 15 days. Visit the Ministry of Foreign Affairs website (www.mfa.go.th) to view eligibility. Visas on arrival are also available for some nationalities. Tourist visas, applied for at consulates or embassies outside of Thailand, generally allow for longer stays of three to six months.

Customs and VAT
Travelers are permitted to bring up to 200 cigarettes (or 250 g/ 900 ounces of tobacco or cigars) and a liter of alcohol into Thailand. Many goods purchased in Thailand qualify for a VAT refund. When you shop, look for stores that display the "VAT Refund For Tourists" sign.

Tourist Offices
The official Tourism Authority of Thailand (TAT) office is located in Phuket Town. All major tourist areas have designated tourist police to ensure that your visit is as safe and pleasant as possible. For tourist police assistance, call 1155. ✆ Tourism Authority of Thailand: 73–5 Phuket Road, Phuket • Map P5 • 07621 2213 • www.tourismthailand.org

Time Differences
Thailand is 12 hours ahead of Eastern Standard Time and 7 hours ahead of Greenwich Mean Time. The country does not observe daylight saving time.

Electrical Appliances
Electricity in Thailand is 220 volts, 50 Hz C. Many wall sockets are designed for flat prongs, such as those from the US and Japan, as well as round prongs, such as those from European and Asian countries. Visitors are advised to bring their own adapters and converters, although both can be purchased on Phuket.

Language
Thailand's official language is Thai, which features five tones and an alphabet that reads from left to right. Regional Thai dialects are still spoken, although central Thai is considered the official version. Although English is widely spoken in most tourist areas, learning a few basic words of Thai will help cultivate good relations with your local hosts.

Preceding pages **Fruit and vegetable market, Phuket Town**

Left **A *tuk-tuk* In Phuket Town** Center **Plane descending near Nai Yang beach** Right **Tourist bus**

Getting There and Around

By Plane
Phuket International Airport (HKT) receives many daily direct flights from overseas, and an even greater number of connecting flights from Bangkok, about 90 minutes away. Direct flights arrive from as far as North America and Europe. The airport is located in the northern part of the island, about 45 minutes away from the major southern beaches.

By Sea
A number of luxury cruise lines dock in Phuket's port for a day or two before continuing to other popular southeast Asian destinations like Penang and Malacca, in Malaysia, and Singapore. Domestic boats arrive from Ko Phi Phi, from islands in the Andaman Sea, and from Phang Nga Bay.

By Bus
Sarasin Bridge links Phuket with the mainland. Buses and minivans between Bangkok and Phuket take around 12 hours. VIP seats on buses and minivans offer the most comfortable ride. Alternatively, trains connect Bangkok to Surat Thani, from where a 6-hour bus ride connects travelers to Phuket.

Taxis
Metered taxis are not widely used on Phuket. Even at the airport, fares are generally determined according to which area you are going to. More frequently, travelers end up bartering for private car services. There is no way to know if you're getting a fair price, so it is best to ask around before agreeing to a fare.

Songthaew
An inexpensive way of traveling between towns is the *songthaew*, literally, "two rows," which has two rows of center-facing benches running down the sides of a pickup truck. Rides start from about B15 per person for short distances. Rides from Phuket Town to various beaches cost about B40–80 per person.

Tuk-Tuk
Unlike in Bangkok, where the familiar three-wheeled vehicle is ubiquitous, *tuk-tuks* are no longer used on Phuket. However, what are often referred to as *tuk-tuks* on the island are actually small red trucks with open sides, almost like miniature *songthaew*. Again, prices have to be negotiated beforehand.

Motorbike Taxis
A fast and easy way to cover short distances is the motorbike taxi; these are easily distinguished by their drivers' brightly colored vests. The taxis congregate mostly in the island's densely populated areas, such as Phuket Town and Patong. The cost per person starts at around B20. As with most public transportation, negotiate a price beforehand.

Motorbike Rental
This cost-effective way of seeing Phuket also gives you the scope to travel as you please. Rentals generally start at around B200 per day for an automatic bike. It is best to be cautious while driving – always wear a helmet and ride very slowly since this is a high-risk way of traveling.

Car Rental
If you plan to travel widely on Phuket, you might want to consider renting a car. Rates start around B1,200 per day during the peak season, but are cheaper during the low season. Reputable agencies are located at the airport, within walking distance of the airport, and also in Phuket Town.

Boats
Long-tail boats can be chartered along the east coast to visit the islands in Phang Nga Bay, while large passenger ferries and speedboats depart from the main piers (Chalong and Bang Rong). The boat drivers usually post their rates on signboards, but these are negotiable. The cost should be roughly B500 per hour.

Left **Sign for Tourist Police** Center **Warning sign at a beach** Right **Pharmacy in Phuket Town**

🔟 Security and Health

Emergencies

In the event of an emergency, dial 191 for the police, or 1155 for the special tourist police. Both offer English-speaking operators. The island does not have an official ambulance service, so visitors who require immediate medical attention should take a taxi or private car to the hospital.

Police

If you require police assistance during your trip, call the Thai police on 191. Alternatively, a special branch of Tourist Police is available 24 hours a day, 7 days a week. These policemen are specially trained volunteers who speak many foreign languages.
🌐 www.phuket-tourist-police-volunteers.com

Hospitals

Phuket International Hospital and Bangkok Phuket Hospital are two of the top-rated hospitals on Phuket and provide western-quality medical care. There are a number of smaller clinics on the island that can treat you for minor illnesses and injuries. Reliable medical care is not available on some smaller islands.

Pharmacies

Thailand's pharmacies sell a wide range of prescription drugs, including many popular Western medicines. Buying drugs in Thailand often does not require a doctor's prescription, so make sure you know the correct dosage before you begin taking a medicine. It is always a good idea to talk to your doctor before taking any medication.

Insurance

Buying insurance is a good idea to cover yourself for private health care, loss of belongings, and cancellations. Although medical care in Thailand is generally inexpensive, insurance gives you peace of mind for unexpectedly large claims. Remember to keep receipts and other documents to file with your insurer when you return home.

Red Flags

When you see red flags flying at the beach, it means you shouldn't enter the water because of strong waves or undertow. These conditions occur most frequently during summer, but you should heed the warning throughout the year, even if other people are ignoring it. Most beaches do not have professional lifeguards.

Motorbikes

Thousands of motorbike accidents occur each year on Phuket, with many riders getting seriously injured. You should always insist that the rental company provide you with a properly fitting helmet. Always obey traffic laws and drive slowly since the margin for error on a motorbike is very thin.

Seasickness

If you experience seasickness, or motion sickness, avoid boat journeys altogether or buy an over-the-counter drug like Dramamine to help control it. You can also mitigate the effects of seasickness by standing on the highest level of the vessel, breathing in fresh air, and fixing your eyes on the horizon.

Sunburn

Sunburn is possible even on cloudy days. The hottest part of the day, from 11am to 2pm, presents the greatest chance for getting burned. Always make sure you wear sunscreen, and reapply it every few hours when you are outside. If you do get burned, you can buy aloe vera and other moisturizers to help alleviate the pain.

Liability

Unlike in most Western countries, the concept of liability is virtually non-existent in Thailand – if you get injured, there is very little you can do. For this reason, it is always a good idea to ask tour operators about their track record and safety precautions before participating in activities.

Left **Post office, Phuket** Center **Tourists exchanging money** Right **Internet café**

10 Banking and Communications

Currency
The local currency is the Thai baht. Foreign currency is generally not accepted. The baht comes in B20, B50, B100, B500 and B1000 paper notes, and B1, B2, B5, and B10 coins. Larger bank notes can be exchanged for smaller denominations at restaurants and major convenience stores.

ATMs
Cash machines can be found throughout Phuket. Some of the smaller islands do not have ATMs so you should withdraw cash before traveling there. It is a good idea to contact your bank to find out how much they charge for foreign transaction fees. Bank ATMs often give better exchange rates than local shops.

Currency Exchange
You can change currency at most banks, currency exchange shops, tourist offices, and hotels. Big banks generally offer the best rates, while tourist offices and hotels should be used only for emergencies. Only exchange with street vendors if you are feeling charitable. Shop around for the best rates, and make sure that commission is included.

Credit Cards
Major hotels and restaurants accept credit cards, but many smaller tour companies do not. Do check with your bank to ask about foreign transaction fees for credit cards, because they are often significant. It is also a good idea to keep the issuing bank's phone number handy in case the card gets lost or stolen.

Money Transfers
A last resort for getting cash (because it is the most expensive), money transfers can be made through Western Union or MoneyGram, giving you instant access to cash. Many banks, post offices, and tourist shops offer these services. Make sure you inquire about commissions and fees before completing the transaction.

Postal Services
Thailand's postal services are generally reliable. You can send important documents or packages via registered airmail or EMS from Thai post offices. Most post offices are open 8am–4:30pm and can assist you with packing boxes and materials. Other major couriers include FedEx and DHL.

Internet Access
WiFi is common at the island's hotels, restaurants, and coffee shops, while Internet cafés are popular throughout the major tourist areas. They usually charge around B1 or 2 per minute. One way to save money on international long-distance calls is to use an Internet-based phone provider, like Skype.

Cell Phones
Thailand's mobile telecommunications infrastructure is very well developed. If you own a GSM phone and your international roaming is activated, your friends and family can easily call your phone number. However, roaming costs can be high. Alternatively, you can buy a local SIM card, which will give you access to a Thai number.

Telephone Cards
If you just want to make outbound calls, and want to avoid paying the rates offered by your hotel, you can buy phone cards at 7-Eleven or other convenience stores. One popular international calling card is the "Tuk Dee." Rates are generally a few baht per minute to North America and Europe.

Dialing Codes
Thailand's country code is 066. When calling Thailand from another country, omit the first 0 included in the region code, after the country code. Within Thailand, there is no need to dial the country code, but you must dial the first 0 in the region code before dialing the rest of the number.

Left **Plaque, Tourist Information Center** Center *Phuket Gazette* Right **Booth at Phuket airport**

TOP 10 Sources of Information

1 Tourism Authority of Thailand

The website of the official government tourism agency, Tourism Authority of Thailand *(see p102)*, offers detailed travel information on destinations throughout Thailand, including Phuket. The agency provides valuable insights into the island's hotels, transportation services, activities, attractions, and more.

2 National Park Visitor Centres

Khao Phra Thaeo National Park *(see pp16–17)*, Sirinat National Park *(see pp18–19)* and Khao Sok National Park *(see pp26–9)* have helpful visitor centers that provide maps, guides, and other useful services. The Department of National Parks also maintains an English version of their website with information on planning trips.
🔊 www.dnp.go.th

3 Websites

A number of well-maintained websites provide up-to-date and candid reviews of Phuket. One of the best developed of these sites, www.phuket.com, features a trove of information about the island's beaches, restaurants, nightlife, and more.

4 Local Newspapers

The English-language newspaper, *Phuket Gazette,* has a well-maintained website with breaking news, upcoming events listings, property listings, and more. The newspaper can be found at hotels, convenience stores, and newsstands in Phuket's busier tourist areas. Visitors can also pick up the *Bangkok Post* and *The Nation*, which are both based in Bangkok.

5 Hotel Concierge

If staying at an upscale hotel, you can ask your concierge to recommend interesting activities. Besides being a source of valuable information, concierge staff can also often secure the best seats at restaurants, or for shows like the Phuket Fantasea *(see p76)*. Many hotels create tours exclusively for their guests.

6 Television

Most hotel rooms have access to CNN or BBC, which provide global weather updates. Thailand does not have its own English TV station, but many hotels provide weather updates, upcoming events, and local features on their in-house programming.

7 Radio

Established in 2008, Phuket FM Radio is the island's English-language radio station. Found on 91.5FM, it provides local news, popular music, weather updates, and entertainment. The radio also streams live online. Broadcasting seven days a week, it can be heard throughout Phuket, as well as on Ko Phi Phi *(see pp92–9)*. 🔊 www.phuketfmradio.com

8 Weather Reports

When planning a day out, it is a good idea to check the weather forecast beforehand, especially during the rainy season. Downpours can occur with little warning. Weather forecasts are available on TV, radio, or the Internet, or best of all, ask a local. The Thai have an uncanny sense of knowing when it will rain.

9 Maps

Complimentary maps are available in the arrival hall at Phuket International Airport. These include detailed maps of each major beach area, as well as a good-quality map of the island's attractions. Street maps of Phuket can also be bought at bookstores and convenience stores on the island.

10 Fellow Travelers

Thailand attracts many long-term and repeat visitors who are often eager to share their travel experiences. Ko Phi Phi draws a huge, mostly young, crowd of backpackers. These travelers are generally fond of swapping advice on cultural or experiential highlights.

Left Sunbathing at Kata beach Right **Night market in Phuket**

10 Things to Avoid

1 Touts
Ignore strangers who approach you offering to sell goods such as gems, or drive you somewhere. These friendly locals often seem like they have your best interests at heart, but they are almost always making a big profit from your credulity.

2 Motorbikes in Unsuitable Conditions
If you rent a motorbike, avoid driving at night or when it is raining. The roads become slick during precipitation and even the slightest error, such as pressing the front brake instead of the rear brake when riding downhill, can spell disaster. Similarly, at night you might not be able to see bumps or sandy patches in the road.

3 Tap Water
It is best not to drink tap water on Phuket. Some high-end hotels purify their water systems, but visitors should generally avoid drinking from taps. It is much safer to drink bottled water provided by your hotel, or purchased from a convenience store. Note that ice cubes at most restaurants and roadside food stalls are made with purified water.

4 Pickpockets
Visitors should beware of pickpockets in crowded spaces such as night markets and tourist streets. Women should always carry their purses and bags in front of their bodies, and keep the zippers closed. Men should move their wallets into their front pockets. While such theft is rare, it does occur occasionally.

5 Theft
It is best not to leave valuables in your hotel room. When possible, use safety deposit boxes for passports, jewelry, cameras, and other valuables. Theft is very rare at upscale hotels, and the front desk can often provide reliable safekeeping. At cheaper guesthouses, security often has lesser control over who enters and leaves the premises.

6 Sunburn
Even on cloudy days, the tropical sun burns hot, so do not forget to apply sunscreen – nothing ruins a holiday faster than sunburn. If you want to work on your tan, the sun's rays are usually strong enough in the mid-morning and late afternoon. Enjoy the hot midday hours in the shade.

7 Unplanned Hiking and Camping
You should always consult with a national park's visitor center before embarking on a trekking or camping trip. These centers can provide maps and other important information for enjoying a safe journey. Also be sure to check the weather forecast, and remember that weather conditions can change quickly so pack for all eventualities.

8 Rainy Season
Even the months with the heaviest rain have long periods of sunshine in Phuket, but the odds of losing a few days to bad weather increase drastically during this time. The upside, however, is that there are fewer visitors and larger discounts.

9 Dubious Establishments
Skin trade thrives on Phuket, particularly in Patong. However, it is quite easy to avoid these establishments. Exercise a degree of caution when entering any bar, nightclub, or massage parlour that has scantily clad girls, or photos of such girls, outside. Also avoid bars where touts try to convince you to enter.

10 Long Road Trips at Night
The hilly and winding coastal roads around Patong are difficult to navigate, even in the best conditions. If your hotel is in Patong and you want to watch the sunset at Naiharn, you should plan to return to Patong before dark, or consider spending the night at Naiharn.

Left **Decorated entrance to the Jui Tui Shrine** Right **Shopping for fruit at a local stall**

🔟 Budget Tips

1 Shopping for Hotels

In densely populated tourist areas, you can visit guesthouses on foot to find the best deal. Always ask to see the room before agreeing to stay there. It is possible to get a steep discount if you arrive late in the afternoon, since the room is likely to remain unoccupied if you do not take it.

2 Local Food

Some of Phuket's most delicious food, usually costing a fraction of what you would pay at a cheap restaurant, can be found on the streets. A good rule of thumb for street food: the more locals eating there, the better. Some vendors have English signs; if not, just point and smile.

3 Market Shopping

Plenty of good deals can be found in the island's night markets. You can save a lot of money if you shop for souvenirs here instead of the air-conditioned malls or boutique stores. Quality T-shirts, beachwear, wood-carvings, and more can be found at affordable prices. Night markets are everywhere on Phuket.

4 Long-term Stays

At small guesthouses, staying for longer than one night often proves to be a good bargaining chip for discounting the room rate. At big hotels or resorts, you will probably need to stay a week before the owner reduces the cost. Monthly rates at apartments or small hotels are much lower than nightly rates.

5 Renting a Motorbike

You can cut down on transportation costs by renting a motorbike from a hotel or tourist shop. Rates start at around B200 per day. Not only are motorbikes cheaper, but they also give you flexibility in terms of time spent at places. The rental company will usually hold your passport as collateral.

6 Free Attractions

Most of the best things on Phuket are free, such as the feel of the sunshine, walking across the soft white sand, and wading in turquoise waters, so maximize your enjoyment of these activities. Other free attractions include visits to Buddhist temples and Chinese shrines, and scenic walks.

7 Staying Inland

Beachfront hotels and rooms with beach views cost more than rooms inland. Remember that you can visit the beach from sunrise to sundown, and slash your daily room costs by spending nights inland. From some rooms you can hear the waves crashing onto the shore, but these rooms come at steep cost.

8 Flying into Bangkok

If you have time to spare, flying into Bangkok and traveling overland to Phuket can save a significant amount of money. Alternatively, you can try some of Thailand's low-cost airlines, such as AirAsia, 1-2-Go, and Nok Air, which offer regular flight services between Bangkok and Phuket. These flights are often much cheaper than the major carriers.

9 Bargaining

Remember that prices for almost everything are negotiable. When a tour operator shows you a glossy brochure with prices, those are normally just the starting point for negotiations. Ask for discounts and check with other merchants for price quotes. Even smaller guesthouses will reduce their nightly rates if you bargain a bit.

10 Reduced Admissions

Many museums, sights, and activities are free; if there is a charge, it is usually reduced for children under 12. When it is not clear, you can simply ask if your child can enter without paying admission, and they might assent. Museums and activities in Thailand do not generally provide special rates for senior citizens or students.

Left Mom Tri's Villa Royale, Kata Noi **Right** Fresh seafood on display at a roadside food stall

10 Accommodations and Dining Tips

1 High and Low Season

Although Phuket can be visited year-round, prices rise during Christmas and New Year. The high tourist season, when prices are higher and rooms should always be reserved in advance, is between November and May. During the low season, which is between June and October, you should inquire about reduced rates at hotels. Many post their rates clearly on their websites.

2 Location

Consider what kind of holiday you want to have on Phuket. If you want activity-filled beaches, bustling crowds, and vibrant nightlife, you should choose one of the southern beaches – such as Patong or Kata – but if you want quiet, natural surroundings, head to a place such as Mai Khao. Phuket's diversity is one of its greatest strengths.

3 Airport Pick-up

Some of Phuket's popular southern beaches are a 45-minute drive from the airport. Many hotels offer free transportation from the airport, if you arrange for it in advance. Not only does this save you from the hassle of dealing with taxi touts, but it also gives you the assurance that you are in the right hands.

4 Hotel Reservation Websites

The Thailand based website, www.agoda. com, has grown to become one of Asia's leading online hotel reservation services. The website offers discounts on hotel rooms, particularly those in the Asia-Pacific region. Another website with a good choice of hotels is www. thailandhotels.net.

5 Confirming Reservations

It is a good idea to email or call the hotel to confirm your reservation before you arrive. Also, if the hotel or travel company has provided you with a confirmation number, you should keep this information handy. Upscale hotels are usually as reliable as hotels in the west, but smaller guesthouses can sometimes be less organized.

6 Street Food

Thailand's street food enjoys a reputation as being one of the most delicious in the world. The food is spicy, sour, tangy, and sweet, and is often prepared in just a few minutes, and to top it all, it is incredibly cheap and very hygienic.

7 Sharing Dishes

Thai food is best eaten when shared by two or more people, with each person getting his or her own plate of rice.

This allows diners to sample many different flavors and textures. Thai salads and soups are usually eaten along with main dishes, a bite of one followed by a bite of another.

8 Vegetarians

Contrary to the food served in Thai restaurants in the West, many of which highlight vegetarian options, the food in Thailand generally includes some sort of meat – most often pork, chicken, or beef. The Thai word for vegan is *ahaan-jay*, and for a vegetarian who eats eggs it is *mahngsawirat*. Food can usually also be specially prepared according to your needs.

9 Eating Utensils

Most Thai food is eaten with a spoon and fork, with the fork being used to guide food on to the spoon. Chopsticks and soupspoons are used for noodle soups. Thai restaurants can also provide knives if needed.

10 Tipping

Many restaurants add a service charge of 10 percent, while some add a 7 percent VAT as well. In general, the custom of tipping in Thailand is to leave whatever coins you receive as change, which usually amounts to anywhere from a few baht up to about B20. You do not need to leave large tips.

Left **Families at a children's park** Right **Kayaking, Phuket**

TOP 10 Specialist Holidays

1 Scuba Diving
The Andaman Sea offers stunning underwater scenery teeming with colorful fish and reefs, as well as crystal-clear waters. Day excursions and live-aboard boats for multi-day trips, depart for popular dive sites, including the Similan Islands. ✆ *Scuba Cat Diving, 94 Thaweewong Road, Patong • 07629 3120 • www.scubacat.com*

2 Cycling
An ideal way to explore rain forests, mountains, and countryside villages, cycling holidays traverse some of Phuket's prettiest back roads and offer an intimate way of experiencing local lifestyles. Tours leave from Phuket to Khao Lak and Khao Sok National Park. ✆ *Amazing Bike Tours Thailand • 07628 3436 • www.amazingbiketours-thailand.asia*

3 Sailing
Sailing enthusiasts throng Phuket for the annual King's Cup Regatta and The Bay Regatta. During the rest of the year, Phuket is a popular hub for sailors who want to explore Phang Nga Bay. Marinas, chartered boat tours, and yacht clubs provide a range of daytrips and overnight journeys. ✆ *Phuket Sail Tours, 199/20 Moo 5, Srisoonthorn, Thalang • 087 897 0492 • www.phuketsailtours.com*

4 Wildlife Watching
The national parks of northern Phuket, Khao Lak, and Khao Sok provide sanctuary to many exotic bird and animal species. Several tour companies offer itineraries geared toward spotting elusive creatures in the wild. ✆ *Paddle Asia, 18/58 Radanusorn • 07624 1519 • Birding day trip: 6:30am–2:30pm daily • www.paddleasia.com*

5 Culinary
From simple sidewalk food stalls serving basic Thai-style fried noodles to upscale white-tablecloth restaurants overlooking the sea, Phuket represents a veritable foodie paradise in Southern Thailand. The island also offers a number of schools where you can learn to cook Thai food.

6 Kayaking
See the wonderful lagoons of Phang Nga Bay by kayak – visit enchanting aquatic grottoes, or join an overnight trip where you camp on an uninhabited island. Some tours explore the mangrove forests along Phuket's coasts. ✆ *John Gray's Sea Canoe, 124 Soi 1 Yaowarat Road, Phuket Town • 07625 4505-7 • www.johngray-seacanoe.com*

7 Spiritual Vacations
Although not generally considered a "spiritual" destination, Phuket does have plenty of soul-seeking opportunities. Many high-end hotels offer yoga classes, while meditation retreats are held at local centers. Watch monks at Buddhist temples perform timeless ceremonies, or join a meditation retreat.

8 Family Vacations
Many hotels in Phuket hotels are child-friendly – they feature special kids clubs, pools and supervisors. With its numerous beaches, golf courses, water parks, tennis courts and venues such as Phuket Fantasea *(see p76)*, the island is a great place for family travel.

9 Honeymoons
As a honeymoon destination, Phuket boasts spectacular beauty: white sand beaches, palm trees, emerald waters, and an extensive choice of resorts, bungalows, and private villas. Few places in the world offer as much romantic possibility, coupled with such good facilities, as Phuket.

10 Rock Climbing
Whether you are an amateur or a veteran cliffhanger, the limestone rock formation on Ko Phi Phi has scenic routes for climbers of all levels. The routes are well-maintained and there is a climbing course for beginners. ✆ *Spidermonkey Climbing, Loh Dalum Bay, Ko Phi Phi • 07560 1026 • www.spidermonkeyphiphi.com*

Left **Shoes outside a shrine** Center **Billboard featuring the king** Right **Devotees praying at a shrine**

10 Etiquette Tips

1 The King
Revered throughout the country, the Thai king is considered to be semi-divine. His portrait appears in many public places, including on the nation's currency. Visitors should be careful not to offend the monarchy since Thailand enforces strict *lese majeste* laws. In fact, it is a social taboo for foreigners to discuss the king in any regard.

2 Removing Shoes
Do remove your shoes at all Buddhist temples, Thai homes, and any other place where you notice a pile of shoes outside the entrance. Thai custom considers feet the dirtiest and lowliest part of the body; the opposite of the head, which is the most respected.

3 The Head
You should refrain from touching Thai people's heads, since it is considered the highest or most respected part of their body. This even applies to young children. Even though it is customary in the West to playfully touch children on the head, in Thailand this can be considered rude or insensitive.

4 Be Careful With Your Feet
Ensure that you do not point with your toes or show someone the sole of your foot. Likewise, if

you drop paper currency, which features the king's portrait, don't step on the money to keep it from blowing away.

5 Respect Buddha Images
Generally it is okay to take photographs of Buddha images, but refrain from pointing your finger directly at the image. When you sit in front of a Buddha image, be careful not to point your toes toward it. Sit cross-legged, or with your legs to one side, pointing backwards.

6 The Wai
The traditional Thai greeting is made by pressing one's hands together just below the chin. It looks similar to the Western prayer gesture. Many Thais, especially businessmen, are accustomed to shaking hands nowadays, but most hotel staff and other Thais will greet you with a *wai*. It is usually polite to *wai* in return.

7 Apologies
If you offend a Thai, you can apologize by making the *wai* gesture to that person. He will usually accept your apology after that, and the episode will have passed. This can smooth over trivial offences, such as bumping into someone in the street, or serious offences, such as verbal altercation.

8 Control Your Temper
Thai culture encourages even-headedness. You often hear Thais say, *mai pen rai*, which roughly means "never mind", "no problem" or "it is not important." Disagreements or mistakes should not lead to raised voices. Losing your temper is considered a loss of face, and it is frowned upon.

9 The Thai Smile
Thailand is known as the "Land of Smiles," but not every smile is the same. Thais smile not only when they are happy, but also when they are embarrassed, amused, wrong, annoyed, or uncertain. Sometimes foreigners mistakenly believe that Thai people are smiling at them, or making fun of them, when they are actually smiling because they are confused or embarrassed.

10 Dress
Although in Western culture revealing clothes are acceptable, in Thailand they can be considered disrespectful or distasteful. In the major tourist areas, local Thais are generally accustomed to foreigners's casual clothes such as bikinis, tank tops, and short shorts. However, if you visit sacred places, like a temple or a Thai person's home, you should dress more conservatively.

Streetsmart

Left **A bird's-eye view of Sri Panwa hotel** Right **The Similan Suite in Anantara Phuket Villas**

TOP 10 Luxury Hotels

1 Sala Phuket Resort & Spa

This ultra stylish boutique resort on Mai Khao Beach is set in gorgeous natural surroundings with five-star facilities. The design marries a classic Phuket architectural style with all modern conveniences. ✆ *333 Moo 3, Mai Khao Beach • Map B2 • 07633 8888 • www.salaresorts. com • BBBB*

2 Anantara Phuket Villas

High levels of privacy and comfort await at these private villas. Rooms feature sliding glass doors that open directly onto your own private swimming pool, while tall fences and greenery ensure maximum seclusion. ✆ *888 Moo 3, Mai Khao Beach • Map B2 • 07633 6100 • www.phuket. anantara.com • BBBBB*

3 JW Marriott Phuket Resort and Spa

Rated as one of Asia's top luxury resorts, the Marriott was among the first high-end properties to develop along Phuket's northwest coast. The rooms feature wooden floors, silks, and plush bedding. ✆ *231 Moo 3, Mai Khao Beach • Map B2 • 07633 8000 • www. marriott.com • BBBB*

4 Six Senses Yao Noi Beyond Phuket

Located on a picturesque island, this luxury hide-away features lush tropical gardens. Each of the 54 sumptuous villas has its own pool. The resort also offers a range of excursions and activities. ✆ *56 Moo 5, Ko Yao Noi • Map F3 • 07641 8500 • www. sixsenses.com • BBBBB*

5 Zeavola

This luxury resort is situated on Ko Phi Phi Don's northern tip. The guest rooms are fashioned out of rich Thai teakwood, and the beds feature cool linens. The resort offers a speedboat transfer service from Phuket. ✆ *Moo 8 Laem Tong, Ko Phi Phi • Map L4 • 07562 7000 • www.zeavola.com • BBBBB*

6 Amanpuri

Graceful, traditional Thai architecture harmonizes with the magnificent tropical surroundings at this luxurious resort. Guest villas come in Thai-style pavilions, pool pavilions, and villa homes. Located on the exclusive Pansea Beach, Amanpuri has top-rated restaurants, such as the French-Japanese Naoki. ✆ *Pansea Beach • Map A6 • 07632 4333 • www.amanresorts. com • BBBBB*

7 The Surin Phuket

This luxury resort boasts 108 well-appointed cottages scattered around the beach and coconut groves. The cottages have handcrafted teak-wood floors, private verandas, and secluded sun decks. Located on Pansea Bay, The Surin enjoys spectacular views ✆ *118 Moo 3, Pansea Beach • Map A6 • 07662 1580 • www.thesurinphuket.com • BBBBB*

8 The Sarojin

Developed in an Asian design style, this luxury resort boasts 56 guest residences. Sheltered by Pakarang Cape, a coral headland, the resort's beach offers calm swimming conditions year-round ✆ *60 Moo 2 Kukkak, Takuapa, Phang Nga • Map E2 • 07642 7900-4 • www. sarojin.com • BBBBB*

9 Sri Panwa

With breathtaking views from atop Panwa Cape, Sri Panwa's villas are set amid lush tropical surroundings. They are designed in a contemporary tropical style and many rooms feature 360-degree views. ✆ *31/17 Moo 8, Sakdidej Road • Map K5 • 07637 1000-3 • www.sripanwa. com • BBBBB*

10 Dusit Thani Laguna Phuket

Located in the Laguna Phuket Resort complex, this hotel is set on the attractive Bang Tao Beach. It offers guests access to numerous Laguna facilities, including an 18-hole golf course. ✆ *390/1 Moo 1, Srisoonthorn Road, Cherngtalay • Map B6 • 07636 2999 • www.dusit. com • BBBB*

Price Categories

For a standard, double room per night (with breakfast if included), taxes, and extra charges.

B	under B1,500
BB	B1,500–3,000
BBB	B3,000–4,500
BBBB	B4,500–6,000
BBBBB	over B6,000

The luxurious Amanzi Villa, Paresa

🔟 Boutique Hotels

1 Aleenta Resort & Spa

Located just 20 minutes north of Phuket's airport, Aleenta offers bright and airy guest rooms. For the ultimate in exclusivity, book Aleenta's beachfront villas, which come with a personal butler. 🔊 33 Moo 5, Kok Klooy, Takuatung, Phang Nga • Map E2 • 07658 0333 • www.aleenta.com/phuket • BBBBB

2 Royal Phuket Yacht Club Hotel

The views of Naiharn Bay from this beachfront property are breathtaking, and it is also the only hotel with direct access to the beach. The hotel's signature restaurant, the Regatta, serves five-course gourmet dinners and good wines. 🔊 23/3 Vises Road, Naiharn Beach • Map H5 • 07638 0200 • www.theroyalphuket yachtclub.com • BBBB

3 Impiana Cabana Resort & Spa

This seaside resort enjoys access to the area's night-life venues, fine eateries, and attractions. But when you want to retire somewhere peaceful, the gates to this resort transport you into a true oasis. 🔊 41 Taweewong Road, Patong Beach • Map N2 • 07634 0138 • www.impiana.com • BBB

4 Paresa

Perched atop a cliff overlooking the Andaman Sea and surrounded by trees and flowers, this boutique resort in Kamala features spacious villas. 🔊 49 Moo 6, Layi-Nakalay Road, Kamala • Map G2 • 07630 2000 • www.paresaresorts.com • BBBBB

5 Malisa Villa Suites

The resort's name derives from the Thai word for "jasmine." The rooms, designed to evoke the comforts of home with modern kitchens and comfortable living spaces, open onto private pools. 🔊 40/36 Kata Road, Kata Beach • Map H5 • 07628 4760-4 • www.malisavillas.com • BBBBB

6 Baan Yin Dee

This resort has Thai style architecture and decorative finishes. The rooftop terrace has great views and a fresh breeze, while the pools are perfect for a cool dip. Rooms feature wooden floors and gentle lighting. 🔊 7/5 Muean Ngen Road, Patong Beach • Map N2 • 07629 4103–6 • www.baanyindee.com • BBBB

7 Twinpalms Phuket

The sleek, minimalist rooms in Twinpalms are personalized with local decorative touches and bespoke furniture. The grounds feature imaginative tropical water gardens. 🔊 106/46 Moo 3, Surin Beach Road • Map A6 • 07631 6500 • www.twinpalms-phuket.com • BBBBB

8 Ayara Hilltops

Situated in an exotic garden, Ayara Hilltops has 48 luxury suites that boast great views of the Andaman Sea. Rooms combine classic Thai design materials, such as teakwood and silk, with contemporary finishes and exquisite lighting. 🔊 125 Moo 3, Surin Beach • Map A6 • 07627 1271 • www.ayarahilltops.com • BBBBB

9 Outrigger Phi Phi Island Resort and Spa

The thatched roof bungalows and villas of this resort blend well with Ko Phi Phi's tropical terrain. Interiors feature rich teakwood and comfor-table luxury furnishings. The resort also has a private beach, as well as a pool overlooking Lo Ba Goa Bay and the Andaman Sea. 🔊 97/197-199 Moo 4, Virat Hongyok Road, Ko Phi Phi • Map F3 • 07562 8900 • www.outrigger.com • BBBBB

10 The Old Phuket

Designed in the classic Phuket architectural style that was popular on the island in the 19th century, this charming hotel still retains the glory of the island's tin mining days. The rooms are modern and well appointed; some have private Jacuzzis. 🔊 192/36 Karon Road, Karon • Map H3 • 07639 6353-6 • www.theoldphuket.com • BBB

Left **Rooftop pool, Andara Resort and Villas** Right **Mom Tri's Villa Royale, Phuket**

Romantic Hotels

Trisara Phuket Resort
Located on a private bay and set amongst lush tropical foliage, Trisara offers 39 private pool villas and suites with an emphasis on privacy. Dedicated cooks and service staff cater to your every need. ✆ *60/1 Moo 6, Srisoonthorn Road, Cherngtalay • Map B6 • 07631 0100 • www. trisara.com • BBBBB*

Sawasdee Village Resort & Spa
Designed to resemble a traditional Thai village using teakwood and Thai artifacts, this has been named one of the most beautiful resorts in the country. ✆*38 Katekwan Road, Kata Beach • Map H5 • 07633 0979 • www.phuketsawasdee. com • BBBB*

Katathani Phuket Beach Resort
Situated on the secluded Kata Noi Bay, this stylish, self-contained luxury resort features six out-door swimming pools and half a dozen highly regarded restaurants. ✆ *14 Kata Noi Road, Karon Beach • Map H4 • 07633 0009 • www.katathani.com • BBBBB*

The Pavilions Phuket
The romantic villas at this resort offer either ocean or hillside views, with unparalleled privacy. Rooms have modern Asian interiors with European touches. It also has facilities for weddings. ✆ *31/1 Moo 6, Cherngtalay •Map B6 • 07631 7600 • www.thepavilionsresorts. com • BBBBB*

Indigo Pearl Hotel
This bold property uses raw timber and chic industrial style to stunning effect. Guest rooms feature subtle touches of individual artistry and have gentle lighting. The hotel has received numerous awards for its trend-setting design. ✆ *Nai Yang Beach • Map B4 • 07632 7006 • www. indigo-pearl.com • BBBBB*

Banyan Tree Phuket
Located in the upscale Laguna resorts complex, this marvelously appointed resort exudes romance and charm. Its romantic dinner cruise takes place on Sanya Rak ("Promise of love"), an aptly named vessel for experiencing Phuket's legendary sunset. ✆ *33/27 Moo 4, Srisoonthorn Road, Cherngtalay • Map B6 • 07632 4374 • www. banyantree.com • BBBBB*

Andara Resort and Villas
Set on a gently sloping hillside overlooking the Andaman Sea, this luxury Thai-inspired retreat boasts intimate villas with private pools, and spacious residential suites. The resort's restaurant, Silk, serves Thai cuisine in stylish surroundings. ✆ *15 Moo 6, Kamala • Map G1 • 07633 8777 •www.andaraphuket. com • BBBBB*

JW Marriott Khao Lak Resort & Spa
A popular destination for honeymooners, this beach-front resort north of Phuket features southeast Asia's longest swimming pool. Nearby attractions include waterfalls, parks, and scuba diving sites. ✆ *41/ 12 Moo 3, Khuk Khak, Takuapa, Phang Nga • Map E1 • 07658 4888 • www. marriott.com • BBBBB*

Cape Panwa Hotel
A charming property on Phuket's southeastern coast, this hotel has hosted many Hollywood film stars. The classic Panwa House, now a restaurant, is regularly featured in movies. The hotel also has access to a private beach. ✆ *27 Moo 8, Sakdidej Road, Cape Panwa • Map K5 • 07637 2400 • www. capepanwa.com • BBBB*

Mom Tri's Villa Royale Phuket
This boutique hotel features luxurious rooms decorated with traditional Thai artistic touches. The property's private cruiser, Yacht Royale, provides exclusive day trips to Phang Nga Bay. ✆ *12 Kata Noi Road, Kata Noi Beach • Map H5 • 07633 3568 • www.villaroyalephuket. com • BBBBB*

Price Categories

For a standard, double room per night (with breakfast if included), taxes and extra charges.

B	under B1,500
BB	B1,500–3,000
BBB	B3,000–4,500
BBBB	B4,500–6,000
BBBBB	over B6,000

Swimming pool at the Mangosteen Resort and Spa

Mid-Range Hotels

1 Burasari Patong Boutique Hotel
Named after the rare flower that blooms on the property, this hotel offers tranquility and some rooms decorated in an elegant classic northern Lanna fashion. ✆ 18/110 Ruamjai Road, Patong • Map N2 • 07629 2929 • www.burasari.com • BBB

2 Baan Krating
With a unique jungle setting, Baan Krating offers seclusion and peace. The villas are well appointed, clean, and comfortable. The beach bar overlooks Naiharn Bay. ✆ 11/3 Moo 1, Wiset Road, Rawai, Ao Sane Beach • Map G6 • 07651 0927 • www.baankrating.com • BB

3 Metropole Phuket
The Metropole Phuket offers 248 rooms and suites in Phuket Town. Guests can enjoy traditional Thai-style massages in the spa, or dine at the two restaurants or executive cocktail lounge. ✆ 1 Soi Surin, Montri Road, Phuket Town • Map P5 • 07621 5050 • www.metropolephuket.com • BB

4 Manathai Resort
A stylish boutique hotel on Surin Beach, Manathai blends contemporary architectural design with classic Asian styles, textures, and fabrics. The Chofa Collection Spa here offers a range of therapeutic massages, scrubs, and wraps. ✆ 121 Srisoonthorn Road, Surin • Map A6 • 07627 0900–5 • www.manathai.com • BBB

5 The Royal Palm Beachfront
Smart interiors define the 67 rooms at the Royal Palm, located in the heart of Patong. With a range of facilities, including an outdoor pool and Jacuzzi, a steam room, and a spa, the hotel offers travelers many comforts. ✆ 66/2 Taweewong Road, Patong • Map N1 • 07629 2510–1 • www.theroyal palm.com • BB

6 Kata Palm Resort and Spa
The comfortable rooms in this resort are furnished in Thai wood and fabrics, with hand-carved teak decorations. With Kata and Karon both located nearby, guests are never far from great shopping, dining, and nightlife. ✆ 60 Kata Road, Kata • Map H5 • 07628 4334 • www.katapalmresort.com • BBB

7 Mangosteen Resort and Spa
A peaceful hilltop resort, the Mangosteen enjoys lovely views of the hills, beaches, and bays of Phuket. At night the resort offers a free shuttle service to the nearby Rawai and Naiharn beaches. ✆ 99/4 Moo 7, Soi Mangosteen, Rawai • Map J5 • 07628 9399 • www.mangosteen-phuket.com • BBB

8 Baan Laimai Beach Resort
This resort offers privacy in the heart of Patong. Some rooms feature hardwood floors and Asian-inspired design. The swimming pool encircles an island with sun beds and palm trees, accessed via a charming bridge. ✆ 66 Thaweewong Road, Patong • Map N1 • 07629 2956-9 • www.baanlaimai.com • BBB

9 Print Kamala Resort
With lush surroundings, the property features a garden, a pool, and sea views. Guest rooms are decorated with natural wood furnishings, and brightly colored walls and bed coverings. Some rooms feature private balconies and Balinese-style interiors. ✆ 74/8 Moo 3, Narhad Road, Kamala • Map G1 • 07638 5396–8 • www.printkamalaresort.net • BBB

10 Millennium Resort
Located off the beach in Patong, this resort gets high marks from visitors for its location. It is next to the upscale Jungceylon shopping mall, and surrounded by popular restaurants and vibrant nightlife. Rooms range from simple chic studios to expansive suites. ✆ 199 Rat-Uthit 200 Pee Road, Patong • Map Q1 • 07660 1999 • www.millenniumhotels.com • BBB

Left **On On Hotel, Phuket** Center **Bar, Kata Beach Studio** Right **Rooftop pool, White Sand Resortel**

Budget Hotels

1 Patong Pearl Resortel
Centrally located in Patong, this well-maintained hotel is a comfortable place to unwind in the middle of the busy city. A swimming pool and sun deck makes this a cut above other budget properties. ◈ *13 Sawadirak Road, Patong • Map N1 • 07634 0121 • www.patongpearl. com • BB*

2 On On Hotel
One of Patong Town's oldest hotels, as well as one of its cheapest, the On On Hotel is extremely basic. This is also where a scene from the movie *The Beach* was filmed. ◈ *19 Phang Nga Road, Phuket Town • Map K3 • 07621 1154 • B*

3 White Sand Resortel
The hotel's well-appointed rooms and spacious suites, all with private balconies, come equipped with TVs. The hotel's restaurant is well-known for its fresh seafood, and the property has a rooftop pool. ◈ *3/7 Sawadirak Road, Patong • Map N1 • 07629 6013–8 • www. whitesandpatong.com • BB*

4 Nai Harn Beach Lagoon Resort
With simple but clean rooms, this hotel is a short distance from Nai Harn Beach. If you stay here, it is a good idea to rent a motorbike. There are a few restaurants and

pubs nearby, but a bike would give you easy access to Naiharn, Rawai, and Kata. ◈ *14/29 Moo 1, Rawai, Naiharn Beach • Map N6 • 07638 8058 • www.naiharnbeachlagoon-resort.com • B*

5 Rattana Beach Hotel
This hotel offers rooms close to Karon Beach. Superior rooms have balconies overlooking the pool. Enjoy a cocktail at the poolside bar, or relax inside a pleasant room. ◈ *72/2–5 Patak Road, Karon • Map H4 • 07639 6415–7 • www. rattanabeach.com • BB*

6 Andatel Hotel Patong Phuket
A short distance from the beach, this hotel has classic Thai-style villas and a charming pool that receives sunlight through the day. Rooms are simple but well kept. ◈ *41/9 Rat-Uthit 200 Pee Road, Patong • Map N1 • 07629 0480 • www. andatelhotel.com • BB*

7 Naiyang Beach Resort
Located in the Sirinat National Park, the Naiyang Beach Resort promises a relaxing stay at prices that are tough to beat. The scenery here is memorable – you drive past a rubber plantation on the way to the resort. ◈ *65/ 23–24 Nai Yang Beach Road • Map B3 • 07632 8300 • www.naiyangbeachresort. com • BB*

8 Kata Beach Studio
The modern studios here have kitchens and balconies, allowing guests to feel at home. The rooftop pool and Jacuzzi feature impressive panoramic views. There is also a swanky poolside bar that is open daily until 10pm. ◈ *90/5 Khoktanod Road, Kata • Map H4 • 07633 3323 • www.katabeachstudio. com • B*

9 Hemingway's Hotel
The name of this hotel evokes images of exotic destinations populated by tough characters. The rooms feature rich woods, silk throw pillows, and Buddha images. It is considered good value for money in Patong. ◈ *188/17–20 Phangmuang, Patong • Map N2 • 07636 6200–3 • www. hemingwayshotel.com • B*

10 Deevana Patong Resort & Spa
This secluded 4-star resort, surrounded by tropical gardens, is spread out on 12 acres (5 ha) of land in Patong. On your doorstep, however, are the world's most famous nightlife, fine dining, and entertainment venues. Simple, clean guest rooms are tastefully decorated and quite comfortable. ◈ *43/2 Rat-Uthit 200, Pee Road, Patong • Map N1 • 07634 1414-5 • www. deevanapatong.com • BB*

Price Categories

For a standard, double room per night (with breakfast if included), taxes and extra charges.

B under B1,500
BB B1,500–3,000
BBB B3,000–4,500
BBBB B4,500–6,000
BBBBB over B6,000

A room with a view at the Outrigger Laguna Phuket Beach Resort

Family Hotels

1 Outrigger Laguna Phuket Beach Resort

Offering a park with pools, a waterslide and activities ranging from kayaking to water basketball, this resort is perfect for families. The kids' club offers a roster of daily activities. ◊ 323 Moo 2, Srisoonthorn, Bang Tao • Map B6 • 07632 4352 • www.outrigger thailand.com • BBBB

2 Phuket Graceland Resort and Spa

The resort's Kid's Club gives children a supervised place to play and to watch movies. There is also a bowling alley, swimming pool, and a Jacuzzi. ◊ 190 Thaweewong Road, Patong • Map N1 • 07637 0500 • www.phuketgraceland. com • BBB

3 JW Marriott Phuket Resort and Spa

The Kids Club here offers a club house with toys for the young, and circus training, batik painting, Thai dancing, Yoga, jewelry making, hair beading, and movies for tweens and teens (see p112).

4 Mövenpick Resort and Spa

The Play Zone in this resort is one of the largest on Phuket. Here, children can participate in a variety of supervised activities. ◊ 509 Patak Road, Karon • Map H4 • 07639 6139 • www.moevenpick-hotels. com • BBB

5 Renaissance Phuket Resort and Spa

Surrounded by greenery and featuring a waterslide, the kids' pool at this resort is a favorite. The Kids Club entertains children with movies, puzzles, books, and video games, all supervised by professionals. The grounds are set on a national park. ◊ 555 Moo 3, Mai Khao Beach • Map B2 • 07636 3999 • www. marriott.com • BBBBB

6 Holiday Inn Phuket Resort

With specially designed family and kids' suites, this resort also has an extensive kids' club, designed for children under 12. Club 12, a parent-free zone with Internet, games, movies, and karaoke, is perfect for teenagers. ◊ 52 Thaweewong Road, Patong • Map N2 • 07634 0608-9 • www.phuket.holiday-inn. com • BBB

7 Hilton Phuket Arcadia Resort and Spa

An expansive property with multiple pools and tennis and squash courts, this hotel also operates a Kidz Paradise Club, where professional staff entertains children while parents are off enjoying the resort and beach. ◊ 333 Patak Road, Karon • Map H4 • 07639 6433 • www.hilton. com • BBBB

8 Laguna Holiday Club Resort

An all-suite resort, this is the most kid-friendly option in the sedate Laguna area. The Kids Club organizes painting and mask-making events, treasure hunts, bowling, and an introduction to Thai games and crafts. Kids over eight can take scuba lessons; babysitting facilities available. ◊ 61 Moo 4, Srisoonthorn Road, Cherngtalay • Map B6 • 07627 1888 • www. lagunaholidayclubresort. com • BBBB

9 Le Meridien Phuket Beach Resort

This resort's Penguin Club for kids aged 3–12 years, offers a range of activities. The resort features a mini-golf course, rock-climbing wall, and multiple pools. Kids can also learn Thai dance, cartoon drawing, and how to make ice cream. ◊ 29 Soi Karon Nui, Karon • Map G3 • 07637 0100 • www. starwoodhotels.com • BBBBB

10 Metadee Resort

This chic resort near Kata Yai Beach has rooms in a unique setting – in a garden surrounded by a large pool. Nearly every room enjoys direct pool access. There is a special kids' pool and fitness center. ◊ 66 Kata Road, Kata • Map H4 • 07633 7888 • www.metadee phuket.com • BBBBB

General Index

Page numbers in **bold** type refer to main entries

7-Eleven 99, 105

A

accommodations
  boutique hotels 113
  budget hotels 116
  budget tips 101, 108
  family hotels 117
  luxury hotels 112
  mid-range hotels 115
  romantic hotels 114
  tips 109
After Beach Bar 56, 79
Aleenta Resort & Spa 113
Amanpuri 86, 112
Amulet Market 68
Anantara Phuket Villas 112
Andara Resort and Villas 114
Andatel Hotel Patong Phuket 116
Anita's Reef 24, 93
Apache Beach Bar 56, 98
Aqua Zone Marine Park 65
ATMs 105
ATV touring 61
Aussie Bar 56, 79
Ayara Hilltops 113

B

Baan Krating 115
Baan Laimai Beach Resort 115
Baan Yin Dee 113
Banana Bar 98
Banana Disco 14, 57, 79
Bangla Boxing Stadium 14, 58, 76
Bangla Road 15, 59
Banyan Tree Gallery 87
Banyan Tree Phuket 114
bargaining 69
bars and nightclubs 56–7
Baru 87
The Bay Regatta 49
Beach Bar 56, 79, 98
beaches 40-41
  Ao Sane Beach 20, 21, 78, 115
  Bang Tao Beach 40, 41, 82, 84, 87, 89
  Emerald Beach 78
  Karon Beach 22, 40, 54, 64, 77
  Kata Beach 7, **22–3**, 40, 77
  Kata Noi 22, 40, 42, 77
  Kata Yai 22, 40
  Ko Similan 24, 47, 93, 96
  Laem Singh Beach 47, 82, 84
  Loh Dalum Beach 41, 59, 96
  Long Beach 40, 70
  Mai Khao Beach 18, 19, 41, 45, 46, 64, 82, 85, 86, 87, 89
  Maya Bay 30, 31, 35, 40, 44, 51, 93, 94, 95
  Naiharn Beach 7, **20–21**, 30, 41, 42, 46, 63, 75
  Nai Thon Beach 18, 19, 86
  Nai Yang Beach 18, 19, 86, 88
  Paradise Beach 78
  Patong Beach 14, 40, 47, 54, 58, 62, 65, 75, 78, 81
beaches (cont.)
  Rawai Beach 71, 78, 93
  Surin Beach 41, 47, 86, 89
  Yanui Beach 20, 21, 78
Beacon Reef 24, 25
Big Buddha 42, 50, 51, 74, 77
Blue Canyon Country Club 60, 82, 83
Blue Elephant Restaurant 11
Bora Bora 98
boxing 58
Bua Phut (flower) 27
bungee jumping 61
Burasari Patong Boutique Hotel 115

C

cabaret shows 14, 15, 58
Cable Jungle Adventure Phuket 86
Canal Village 67, 84
Candere Gallery 87
Cape Panwa Hotel 114
Carlito's Bar 98
car rental 103
cell phones 105
Cham, Luan Pho 35
Chan's Antique House 68
Chao Ley Boat Floating Festival 49
Charbonneau Rene 35
Chatuchak Weekend Market 8, 66
Cheow Laan Lake 7, 26, 27, 45, 93
Chevalier de Chaumont, Alexandre 35
children's activities 64–5

Chinese Junk Boat 30, 31
Chinese New Year 9, 36, 48
Chinpracha House 10, 51
Christmas Point 24, 25
cinema 61
credit cards 105
currency 105
customs regulations 102
cycling 60, 110

D
day trips 70–71
Deevana Patong Resort & Spa 116
Desfarges, General Marshal 34
dialing codes 105
Dino Park Mini-Golf 22
discotheques 14
D's Books 99
Dusit Thani Laguna Phuket 54, 89, 112

E
East of Eden 24, 25, 93
Easyriders 79
Edward Miles 35, 51
electricity 102
Elephant Head Rock 24, 25
elephant trekking 16, 17, 22, 23, 26, 60, 88
elephant rides 64, 84
emergencies 104
entertainment venues 58–9
etiquette 111

F
family vacations 110
fairs and festivals 48, 49
  Chao Ley Boat Floating Festival 49
  Chinese New Year 9, 13, 36, 48

fairs and festivals (cont.)
  Loy Krathong 49
  Old Phuket Festival 48
  Phuket Gay Pride Festival 48
  Phuket International Blues Festival 48
  Phuket Vegetarian Festival 8, 9, 38, 49, 74, 75, 78
  Por Tor Festival 48
  Songkran 48
  Visakha Puja 48
  Wat Chalong Fair 13, 36
Fine 9 Design 87
fire dancing 59
fishing 63
flora 16, 17, 29, 46, 82
Flora in Khao Sok 29
food
  cooking classes 23, 97
  dishes 55
  budget tips 101, 108
  dining tips 101, 109
  exotic fruits 67
  local drinks 57
  street food 109
  vegetarian 8, 9, 38, 39, 49, 74, 75, 78, 109

G
Gibbon Rehabilitation Centre 6, 16, 17, 44, 82, 84, 85
Gibbon Rehabilitation Project 16
Ginger Boutique 87
Grand Pagoda 6, 12

H
health 104
helicopter charters 43
Hemingway's Hotel 116
Heritage Collection 87
Heroines' Monument 35, 36, 50, 85, 86

Hilton Phuket Arcadia Resort and Spa 117
historic buildings 10–11
history 34–5
Holiday Inn Phuket Resort 117
honeymoons 110
hospitals 104
hotels see accommodations
House of the Beautiful Images 11

I
Ibiza Bar 98
Impiana Cabana Resort & Spa 113
Indigo Pearl Hotel 114
Internet 105

J
James Bond Island (Ko Phing Kan) 7, 30, 31, 44, 51, 70, 92, 93, 95
Jim Thompson 66, 68
Jungceylon 61, 67, 115
JW Marriott Khao Lak Resort & Spa 114
JW Marriott Phuket Resort and Spa 112

K
Kangaroo Bar 56, 79
Karon 40, 42, 54, 64, 66, 68, 74, 77
Karon Viewpoint 22, 23, 42, 77, 78, 79
Kata 7, **22–3**, 40, 42, 60, 68, 76, 77, 78, 79, 81
Kata Beach Studio 116
Kata Noi 22, 40, 42, 77, 114
Kata Palm Resort and Spa 115
Kata Plaza 66

Katathani Phuket
Beach Resort 114
Kata Yai 22, 40, 117
Kathu Mining Museum
50
kayaking 26, 30, 31, 45,
54, 62, 82, 110
Khao Khad Views
Tower 42
Khao Khian 30, 31
Khao Lak 47, 92, 93,
94, 96, 110, 114
Khao Rang Viewpoint
44
Kin Dee Restaurant 89
King Cruiser Wreck
dive 92, 94
King's Cup Regatta 49
Ko Bon 24, 25, 71
Ko Hae 70, 96
Ko Kaew 71
Ko Khai Nok 71
Ko Maphrao 70
Ko Miang 24
Ko Panyee 30, 31, 51,
70, 92, 93, 95
Ko Phi Phi 7, 30, 31,
35, 44, 51, 57, 59, 60,
61, 94
Ko Phi Phi Don 30, 31,
43, 92, 94, 95
Ko Phi Phi Ley 30, 40,
43, 44, 51, 92
Ko Racha 71, 74
Ko Rang Yai 71
Ko Similan 24, 47, 93,
96
Ko Sirey 9
Ko Yao Noi 30, 31, 70,
96, 112
Ko Yao Yai 70
Kunstone 99
Kun Va 99

L

Laem Singh Beach 47,
82, 84
Laguna Phuket Golf
Club 86

Laguna Phuket
International
Marathon 49
Laguna Phuket
Trilathon 49
languages 102
Le Meridien Phuket
Beach Resort 117
Lemongrass House 87
Light, Captain Francis
35
Lim's Restaurant 81
local travel 103
Loh Dalum Bay 95

M

Mai Khao Marine Turtle
Foundation 18, 19
Malisa Villa Suites 113
Manathai Resort 115
Mangosteen Resort
and Spa 115
mangroves 45
maps 106
merit-making 13
Metadee Resort 117
Metropole Phuket 115
Millennium Resort 115
mini-golf 22, 64, 71
MJ Bamboo Tattoo 99
Molly Malone's 57, 79
Mom Luang Tri
Devakul 35
Mom Tri's Villa Royale
Phuket 114
money 105
Monkey Beach 95, 96
Monkey Hill 8, 9, 43
monuments see
museums
motorbike rides 60
Mövenpick Resort and
Spa 117
movies shot in Phuket
51
Bridget Jones: The
Edge of Reason 51
Casualties of War 51
Cutthroat Island 51

movies shot in Phuket
(cont.)
Good Morning,
Vietnam 51
Heaven and Earth 51
Star Wars: Episode
III Revenge of the
Sith 51
The Beach 30, 31, 35,
40, 51, 93, 94, 116
The Killing Fields 51
The Man with the
Golden Gun 31, 51
Tomorrow Never Dies
51
Muay Thai 14, 15, 20,
21, 49, 74, 76
Muay Thai gyms 21,
76
museums and
monuments 50–51
Big Buddha 42, 50,
51, 74, 77
Kathu Mining
Museum 50
Phuket Cultural
Centre 8, 50
Phuket Philatelic
Museum 11, 50
Phuket Seashell
Museum 50, 69
Phuket Tai Hua
Museum 10, 50
Saphan Hin Mining
Monument 51
Thalang National
Museum 51, 82, 85
Thavorn Lobby Hotel
Museum 51

N

Naiharn 7, **20–21**, 22,
30, 40, 41, 42, 46, 56,
63, 74, 75, 77, 78, 81,
88
Nai Harn Beach
Lagoon Resort 116
Naiharn Buddhist
Monastery 20, 21

Naiharn lake 20, 21, 46, 56, 75, 77
Naiharn village 20, 21
Nai Yang Beach Resort 116
Narai, King 34
national parks
  Khao Phra Thaeo National Park 6, **16–17**, 44, 82, 85, 86, 88
  Khao Sok National Park 7, **26–9**, 44, 45, 47, 60, 92, 93, 106, 110
  Sirinat National Park 6, **18–19**, 45, 83, 106
  Surin Islands National Marine Park 96
  Visitor Centres 106
newspapers 106
nightclubs see bars and nightclubs
night markets 68

O
The Old Phuket 113
Old Phuket Festival 48
On On Hotel 116
outdoor activities 60–61
  ATV touring 61
  bamboo rafting 26, 27
  bicycling 88
  boating 14, 92
  budget tips 101, 108
  bungee jumping 61
  camping 18, 19, 88, 96, 107
  canoeing 26, 88
  children's activities 64, 65
  cycling 60, 110
  deep sea fishing 62
  diving precautions 25
  elephant rides 64, 84
  fishing 63

outdoor activities (cont.)
  go-karting 65
  golf 60, 88
  horseback riding 60, 84, 88
  jet-skiing 62
  jungle trekking 26
  live-aboard boats 24
  marine activities 62, 63
  mini-golf 22
  nature trails 18
  night safaris 26, 27
  outdoor activities in the North 88
  parasailing 14, 40, 62, 77
  road trips 107
  rock climbing 61, 110
  scuba diving 18, 19, 63, 110
  snorkeling 19, 62, 88
  stargazing 96
  sunbathing 60
  surfing 20, 49, 62, 88
  swimming 62, 85, 88
  trekking 16, 17, 22, 23, 26, 60, 88, 92
  walks 18, 46, 47
  water sports 14, 22
  windsurfing 86
Outrigger Laguna Phuket Beach Resort 117
Outrigger Phi Phi Island Resort and Spa 113

P
The Palace of Art 87
Paresa 81, 113
parks & gardens
  King Rama IX Park 9
  Rang Hill 8, 9, 43, 44, 80
  Suan Luang Park 8, 9
passports 102
Patong 6, **14–15**, 47, 75, 77

Patong Boxing Stadium 14, 58, 76
Patong night market 66
Patong Pearl Resortel 116
The Pavilions Phuket 89, 114
Pee Pee Bakery 97
Phang Nga Bay 7, **30–31**, 44, 51, 54, 62, 70, 92, 93, 95, 96, 103
pharmacies 104
Phi Phi Viewpoint 30, 31, 42, 43, 94
Phromthep Cape 7, 20, 21, 42, 44, 45, 46, 57, 76, 77
  market 67
Phuket Aquarium 64, 78
Phuket Bike Week 49
Phuket Boat Lagoon 82, 83, 84
Phuket Butterfly Garden and Insect World 8, 9, 65
Phuket Cultural Centre 8, 50
Phuket Fantasea 58, 64, 74, 76, 106, 110
Phuket Graceland Resort and Spa 117
Phuket International Blues Festival 48
Phuket International Cricket Sixes Tournament 49
Phuket International Rugby Tournament 49
Phuket Orchid Farm 78
Phuket Pearl Factory 69
Phuket Philatelic Museum 11, 50
Phuket Provincial Hall 10
Phuket Seashell Museum 50, 69

Phuket Shooting Range 59, 61, 65
Phuket Surfing Contest 49
Phuket Thai Hua Museum 10, 50
Phuket Town 6, **8–11**, 46, 66, 75, 76, 80
Phuket Wake Park 63
Phuket Zoo 59, 65, 78
shows 59
Playhouse 58
police 104
postal services 105
Pote Sarasin 35
P. P. Marijuana Shop 99
Print Kamala Resort 115
Ptolemy 34

Q

The Quarterdeck 81

R

raft houses 27
Rama V, King 13, 34, 35, 50, 83
Rasita 99
Rassada Pier 95
Ratchaprapha Dam 27, 29
Ratri Italian Bar and Grill 81
Rattana Beach Hotel 116
Red Coral 87
Reggae Bar 79, 98, 99
Renaissance Phuket Resort and Spa 117
restaurants 54–5
  Phuket Town 80
  The South 81
  The North 89
  Farther Afield 97
Rock City 79
Rolling Stoned Bar 57, 98
Roots Rock Reggae Bar 79

The Royal Palm Beachfront 115
Royal Phuket Yacht Club Hotel 113

S

safari 23, 27, 44, 64, 93
sailing 110
Sala Phuket Resort & Spa 112
Same Same 99
The Sarojin 112
Sawasdee Village Resort & Spa 114
scenic spots 44, 45
scuba diving 18, 19, 63, 110
seasons 102
  high and low season 109
  rainy season 107
sea turtles 18, 84
security 104
  pickpockets 107
  theft 107
  touts 107
Seduction Discotheque 14
Sheraton Grande Laguna 117
shopping 66, 67
  bargaining tips 69
  shopping in the North 87
  shopping on Ko Phi Phi 99
  souvenirs 68, 69
  shopping on Ko Phi Phi 99
shows see entertainment venues
Similan Islands 7, **24–5**, 45, 47, 92, 93, 110
Simon Cabaret 15, 58
Six Senses Phuket Raceweek 49

Six Senses Yao Noi Beyond Phuket 112
snake shows 59
Sok River 26
songthaew 103
Soul of Asia 68, 87
spa and massage treatments 22, 23
specialist vacations 110
Splash Jungle Waterpark 64, 86
sporting events 49
Sri Panwa 112
Srisoonthorn, Thao 34, 35
Standard Chartered Bank Building 10
The Stones Bar 98
The Surin Phuket 112

T

tailors (bespoke) 68
Talay Karon Beach Resort 117
taxis (motorbike) 103
telephones
  dialing codes 105
  telephone cards 105
temples
  Bang Niew Shrine 38
  Boon Kaw Kong Shrine 38
  Buddhist Temples 36, 37
  Cherngtalay Shrine 38, 39
  Chinese shrines 8, 9, 38, 39, 46, 78
  Jui Tui Chinese Temple 38
  Kathu Shrine 39
  Kuan Te Kun Shrine 39
  Put Jaw Chinese Temple 38, 39
  Sam San Shrine 38
  Shrine of the Serene Light 38
  Tha Rua Chinese Shrine 39

temples (cont.)
Wat Chalong 6, **12–13**, 36, 75
Wat Kajonrangsan 37
Wat Kathu 37
Wat Kosit Wihan 37
Wat Mai Khao 86
Wat Phranang Sang 36
Wat Prathong 34, 36, 82, 83
Wat Putta Mongkol 37
Wat Srisoonthorn 36
Wat Suwan Khiri Khet 36
Wat Suwan Kuha 37
THAI Airways Office Building 11
Thai Furniture 69
Thalong Road 66
theatres see entertainment venues
Thep Kasattri, Thao 34, 35
Timber Rock 56, 79
time zone 102
Tiger Disco 14
Ton Sai Bay 95
Tourism Authority of Thailand 102, 106
tourist offices 102
transport 103

travel planning 102
trekking 16, 17, 22, 23, 26, 60, 88, 92
Trisara Phuket Resort 114
T-shirts 15, 57, 66, 71, 99, 108
tuk-tuks 103
Turtle Village Shopping Centre 66
Twinpalms Phuket 113

U
Underwater World 30

V
vaccinations 102
Vegetarian Festival 8, 38, 49, 74, 75, 78
Velvet Dojo 56, 98
viewing points 42, 43
Big Buddha Viewpoint 42
Karon Viewpoint 22, 23, 42, 77, 78, 79
Khao Khad Views Tower 42
Khao Rang Viewpoint 44
Monkey Hill 8, 9, 43
Phi Phi Viewpoint 30, 31, 42, 43, 94
Radar Hill Viewpoint 43
Rang Hill 8, 9, 43, 44, 80
Windmill Viewpoint 20, 21, 42

Viking Cave 44, 96
Visakha Puja 48
visas 102

W
walks 18, 46, 47
Wat Chalong Fair 13, 36
waterfalls 26, 86
Bang Pae Waterfall 16, 44, 85, 86, 88
Ton Sai Waterfall 6, 16, 85, 86
water (drinking) 107
water sports 14
weather 106, 107
White Sand Resortel 116
wildlife 16, 17, 26, 27, 46, 60, 106, 110
wildlife in Khao Sok 28, 29
Wildlife Conservation Development and Extension Centre 17
Windmill Viewpoint 20, 21, 42

Y
Yoonique Stone Music Café 56, 79

Z
Zeavola 112

Acknowledgments

The Author
A frequent traveler to Phuket and southern Thailand, William Bredesen has been the assistant editor of *Bangkok Post themagazine* since 2009. He has previously worked on a contemporary Thai history book, *Chronicle of Thailand: Headline News Since 1946*, and he holds a Master's degree in Southeast Asian Studies from Chulalongkorn University in Bangkok.

Photographer: Brent T. Madison

Additional Photography: Peter Anderson, David Henley, Dorota and Mariusz Jarymowiczowie.

At DK INDIA
Managing Editor Madhavi Singh
Editorial Manager Sheeba Bhatnagar
Design Manager Mathew Kurien
Project Editor Parvati M. Krishnan
Project Designer Aradhana Gupta
Assistant Cartographic Manager Suresh Kumar
Cartographer Subhashree Bharati
Maps
Base mapping supplied by Huber Kartographie
Picture Research Manager Taiyaba Khatoon
Senior DTP Designer Azeem Siddiqui
Indexer Andy Kulkarni
Proofreader Amit Kapil

At DK LONDON
Publisher Vivien Antwi
List Manager Christine Stroyan
Senior Managing Art Editor Mabel Chan
Senior Editor Sadie Smith
Editorial Assistance Julie Oughton
Designer Tracy Smith
Cartographer Stuart James
Senior DTP Designer Jason Little
Production Controller Emma Sparks
Revisions Team:
Kate Berens, Peter Holmshaw, Bharti Karakoti, Alison McGill, George Nimmo, Susie Peachey, Ellen Root, Sands Publishing Solutions.

Photography Permissions:
Dorling Kindersley would like to thank the following for their assistance and kind permission to photograph at their establishments:

Chan's Antique House, China Inn Café & Restaurant, D's Books, Kra Jok See, Thungkha Kafae, Rolling Stoned Bar, Yoonique Stone Music Café.

Picture Credits:

(Key: a-above; b-below/bottom; c-center; f-far; l-left; r-right; t-top)

The publisher would like to thank the following for their kind permission to reproduce their photographs:

ALAMY IMAGES: Gary Dublanko 52-53.

ANANTARA HOTELS, RESORTS & SPAS: 112tr.

ANDARA RESORTS AND VILLAS: 114tl.

BAAN RIM PA GROUP: 54tl, 54bl, 81tl.

BANYAN TREE HOTELS & RESORTS: Banyan Tree Gallery 87tr.

BLUE CANYON COUNTRY CLUB: 83b.

CORBIS: Axiom Photographic / Design Pics 90-91, Science Faction / F. Stuart Westmorland 25tl.

CPA MEDIA: 34tl, 34tr, 34cr.

DREAMSTIME.COM: Lee Snider 10tl.

FLPA: Imagebroker / Norbert Probst 25bl.

GETTY IMAGES: AFP / Roslan Rahman 35bl.

GINGER FASHION: 87tl.

GOLDEN TULIP MANGOSTEEN RESORT & Spa: 115tl.

JW MARRIOTT PHUKET RESORT & SPA: 89tl.

KASEMKIJ HOTELS: 112tl.

LAGUNA PHUKET GOLF CLUB: 86tl.

MASTERFILE: Oriental Touch 95cl.

MOM TRI'S BOATHOUSE: 55cl.

MOM TRI'S VILLA ROYALE PHUKET: 109tl, 114tr.

OUTRIGGER LAGUNA PHUKET BEACH RESORT: 117tl.

PARESA RESORTS: 113tl.

PHOTOLIBRARY: Age fotostock/ Dhritiman Mukherjee 28tr; Alamy/ Paul Kennedy 65cl, /Pavlos Christoforou 20br, /Zach Holmes 99tl; Image Source 7bl; Imagebroker.net/JW.Alker 7crb, / Terry Whittaker/FLPA 28cl; Imagestate RM/Steve Vidler 60bl; Oxford Scientific (OSF)/Koshy Johnson 28br; Weimann P 28tl; Picture Press/Andreas Rose 4-5; Robert Harding Travel/Luca Tettoni 70tl; WaterFrame – Underwater Images/Reinhard Dirscherl 25cra; Peter Widmann 31cr.

PHUKET FANTASEA: 58tl, 64tl.

PHUKET RIDING CLUB: 61cla, 88tl.

RATRI JAZZTAURANT: 81tc.

SALA PHUKET RESORT AND SPA: 89tc.

WIKIPEDIA: 35tr.

All other images © Dorling Kindersley. For further information see: *www.dkimages.com*

Phrase Book

Thai is a tonal language and regarded by most linguists as head of a distinct language group, though it incorporates many Sanskrit words from ancient India, and some of modern English ones, too. There are five tones: mid, high, low, rising, and falling. The particular tone, or pitch, at which each syllable is pronounced determines its meaning. For instance "mǎi" (falling tone) means "not," but "mǎi" (rising tone) is "silk." See the Guidelines for Pronunciation for a phonetic transliteration of the Thai script for English speakers, including guidance for tones in the form of accents.

Guidelines for Pronunciation

When reading the phonetics, pronounce syllables as if they form English words. For instance:

a	as in "ago"
e	as in "hen"
i	as in "thin"
o	as in "on"
u	as in "gun"
ah	as in "rather"
ai	as in "Thai"
air	as in "pair"
ao	as in "Mao Zedong"
ay	as in "day"
er	as in "enter"
ew	as in "few"
oh	as in "go"
oo	as in "boot"
OO	as in "book"
oy	as in "toy"
g	as in "give"
ng	as in "sing"

These sounds have no close equivalents in English:

eu	can be likened to a sound of disgust - the sound could be written as "errgh"
bp	a single sound between a "b" and a "p"
dt	a single sound between a "d" and a "t"

Note that when "p," "t," and "k" occur at the end of Thai words, the sound is "swallowed." Also note that many Thais use an "l" instead of an "r" sound

The Five Tones

Accents indicate the tone of each syllable.

no mark	The **mid tone** is voiced at the speaker's normal, even pitch.
á é í ó ú	The **high tone** is pitched slightly higher than the mid tone.
à è ì ò ù	The **low tone** is pitched slightly lower than the mid tone.
ǎ ě ǐ ǒ ǔ	The **rising tone** sounds like a questioning pitch, starting low and rising.
â ê î ô û	The **falling tone** sounds similar to an syllable word for emphasis.

In an Emergency

Help!	chôo-ay dôo-ay!
Fire!	fai mâi!
Where is the nearest hospital?	tâir-o-nêe mee rohng pa-yah-bahn yòo têe-
Call an	rêe-uk rót pa-yah-

ambulance!   bahn hǎi nòy!
Call a doctor!   rêe-uk mǒr hǎi nòy!
Call the police!   rêe-uk dtum ròo-ut hǎi nòy!

Communication Essentials

Yes	châi or krúp/kâ
No	mâi châi or mâi krúp/mâi kâ
Please can you...?	chôo-ay
Thank you	kòrp-kOOn
No, thank you	mâi ao kòrp-kOOn
Excuse me/sorry	kǒr-tôht (krúp/kâ)
Hello	sa-wùt dee (krúp/kâ)
Goodbye	lah gòrn ná

Useful Phrases

How are you?	kOOn sa-bai dee reu (krúp/kâ)?
Very well, thank you	sa-bai dee (krúp/kâ)
How do I get to...?	...bpai yung-ngai?
Do you speak English?	kOOn pôot pah-sǎh ung-grìt bpen mǎi?
I can't speak Thai.	pôot pah-sǎh tai mâi bpenl
Where is the nearest public telephone?	tâir-o nêe mee toh-ra-sùp yòo têe-nǎi?

Useful Words

hot	rórn
cold	yen or nǎo
good	dee
bad	mâi dee
open	bpèrt
closed	bpìt
left	sái
right	kwǎh
near	glâi
toilet	hôrng nǎhm

Shopping

How much does this cost?	nêe rah-kah tâo-rài?
Do you have?	mee...mǎi?
Do you take credit cards/travelers' checks?	rúb but cray-dìt/ chék dern tang mǎi?
What time do you open/close?	bpèrt/bpìt gèe mohng?
Can you ship this overseas?	sòng không nee bpai dtàhng bpra-tâyt dâi mǎi?
Could you lower the price a bit?	lót rah-kah nòy dâi mǎi?
How about...baht?	...bàht dâi mǎi?
I'll settle for...baht.	...bàht gôr lâir-o-gun
Thai silk	pâh-mǎi tai
pharmacy	ráhn kǎi yah
market	dta-làht
supermarket	sOOp-bpêr-mah-gèt

*In polite speech, Thai men add "**krúp**" at the end of each sentence; women add "**ká**" at the end of questions and "**kâ**" at the end of statements*

Staying in a Hotel

Do you have a vacant room?	mee hôrng wâhng mái?
air-conditioned	hôrng air
room	
I'd like a room for one night/three nights.	(pôm/dee-chún) ja pùk yòo keun nèung/ sähm keun
What is the charge per night?	kâh hôrng wun la tâo-rái?
May I see the room first please?	kôr doo hôrng gòrn dâi mái?
Will you spray some mosquito repellent, please?	chôo-ay chèet yah gun yOOng hâi nòy dâi mái?
double/twin room	hôrng kôo
single room	hôrng dèe-o
bill	bin
key	gOOn-jair
shower	fúk boo-a
swimming pool	sá wâi náhm

Sightseeing

tourist office	sûm-núk ngahn gahn tôrng têe-o
tourist police	dtum-ròo-ut tôrng têe-o
beach	hâht or chai-hâht
island (koh)	gòr
museum	pí-pít-ta-pun
national park	ÒO-ta yahn hâirng châht
temple (wat)	wût
Thai boxing	moo-ay tai
Thai massage	nôo-ut
trekking	gahn dern tahng táo

Transportation

How long does it take to get to...?	chái way-lah nahn tâo-rài bpai têung têe-o...?
What station is this?	têe nêe sa-tâhn-nee a-rai?
ticket	dtOo-a
air-conditioned bus	rót bprùp ah-gàht
airport	sa-náhm bin
tour bus	rót too-a
train	rót fai
bus station	sa-tâhn-nee rót may
moped	rót mor-dter-sai
taxi	táirk-sêe

Eating Out

A table for two please.	kôr dtó sûm-rúp sôrng kon
May I see the menu?	kôr doo may-noo nòy?
Do you have...?	mee...mái?
Is it spicy?	pèt mái?
May I have a glass of water, please.	kôr núm kâirng bplào gâir-o nèung
Waiter/waitress!	kOOn (krúp/kâ)
The check, please.	kôr bin nòy (krúp/kâ)

Menu Decoder

néu-a woo-a	beef
bee-a	beer
yâhng	char-grilled
gài	chicken
prík	chili
gah-fair	coffee
bpoo	crab
mèe gròrp	crispy noodles
gôo-ay dtêe-o hâirng	dry noodles
bpèt	duck
tOO-ree-un	durian
kài	egg
bplah	fish
kíng	ginger
núm kâirng bplào	iced water
hèt	mushroom
gôo-ay dtêe-o-náhm	noodle soup
ma-la-gor	papaya
súp-bpa-rót	pineapple
néu-a-môo	pork
kâo	rice
gôo-ay dtêe-o	rice noodles
gÔOng	shrimp
ah-hâhn wâhng	soy sauce
núm chah	tea
pùk	vegetables
náhm	water

Health

I do not feel well	róå-sèuk mâi sa-bai
I have a fever.	dtoo-a-rórn bpen kâi
asthma	rôhk hèut
diabetes	rôhk bao wâhn
diarrhea	tórng sêe-a
dizzy	wee-un hôo-a
stomach ache	bpòo-ut tórng
fever	kâi
aspirin	air-sa-bprin or yah- gàir kâi
doctor	môr
dentist	tun-dta-pâirt or môr fun
hospital	rohng pa-yah-bahn
medicine	yah
prescription	bai sùng yah
I'm allergic to...	(pôm/dee-chún) páir...

Numbers

0	sŏon
1	nèung
2	sŏrng
3	sähm
4	sèe
5	hâh
6	hòk
7	jèt
8	bpàirt
9	gâo
10	sìp
100	nèung róy
one hour	nèung chôo-a mohng
half an hour	krêung chôo-a mohng
Sunday	wun ah-tít
Monday	wun jun
Tuesday	wun ung-kahn
Wednesday	wun pOOt
Thursday	wun pa-réu-hùt
Friday	wun sÒOk
Saturday	wun săo

Selected Sight Index

Amulet Market	P5
Ao Sane Beach	H6
Bang Niew Shrine	Q6
Bang Pae Waterfall	D5
Bangla Boxing Stadium	Q1
Big Buddha Viewpoint	H4
Blue Canyon Country Club	C3
Boon Kaw Kong Shrine	H2
Cable Jungle Adventure Phuket	D5
Canal Village	B6
Chan's Antique House	J2
Chatuchak Weekend Market	P5
Cherngtalay Shrine	B6
Chinpracha House	N5
Christmas Point	D2
Dino Park Mini-Golf	H4
Emerald Beach	G3
Gibbon Rehabilitation Centre	D5
Heroines' Monument	C6
James Bond Island	F3
Jui Tui Chinese Temple	N5
Jungceylon	P2
Karon Viewpoint	H5
Kata Beach	K4
Kathu Mining Museum	J2
Khao Khad Views Tower	K4
Khao Phra Thaeo National Park	D5
Khao Sok National Park	F1
Khao Khian	F3
Ko Hae	J6
Ko Kaew	H6
Ko Maphrao	L2
Ko Panyee	F2
Ko Phi Phi Ley	F4
Ko Rang Yai	L1
Ko Yao Noi	F3
Kuan Te Kun Shrine	K
Laem Singh Beach	G1
Laguna Phuket Golf Club	B6
Loh Dalum Beach	L6
Long Beach	M6
Mangrove Forest	B1
Monkey Beach	L5
Naiharn Beach	H6
Naiharn Buddhist Monastery	H5
Naiharn Lake	H5
Paradise Beach	G3
Patong Boxing Stadium	P1
Patong Go-Kart Speedway	H2
Phuket Pearl Factory	Ł1
Phang Nga Bay	F
Phromthep Cape	H
Phuket Philatelic Museum	P
Phuket Aquarium	K
Phuket Boat Lagoon	K
Phuket Butterfly Garden and Insect World	K
Phuket Cultural Centre	K:
Phuket Fantasea	G
Phuket Orchid Farm	J
Phuket Provincial Hall	Q
Phuket Seashell Museum	H
Phuket Shooting Range	J
Phuket Thai Hua Museum	P
Phuket Zoo	J
Put Jaw Shrine	N
Rawai Beach	H
Rawai Muay Thai	H
Sam San Shrine	N
Saphan Hin Mining Monument	K:
Sea Turtle Laying Point	B.
Shrine of the Serene Light	P
Siam Safari	J
Similan Islands	D
Sirinat National Park	B.
Soul of Asia	K
Splash Jungle Waterpark	B.
Tha Rua Chinese Shrine	J
THAI Airways Office	P
Thai Furniture	J
Thalang National Museum	D
Thavorn Lobby Hotel Museum	P
Ton Sai Waterfall	D
Turtle Village Shopping Centre	B.
Wat Chalong	J
Wat Kajonrangsan	N
Wat Kosit Wihan	K:
Wat Phranang Sang	C
Wat Prathong	C
Wat Putta Mongkol	P
Wat Srisoonthorn	C
Wat Suwan Khiri Khet	H
Wildlife Conservation Development and Extension Centre	D
Windmill Viewpoint	H
Yanui Beach	H